A manual on counselling

JEHOVAH'S WITNESSES

by JOHN CAMPBELL

ISBN 0 946351 27 9

A MANUAL ON COUNSELLING
JEHOVAH'S WITNESSES
Copyright © 1991 by John Ritch
40 Beansburn, Kilmarnock, Sco.

About the Author

Born in Wigtownshire and converted there John Campbell moved with his parents to Ayr in his teens. Here he acquired a love for the scriptures and a zeal for the gospel. Sometimes alone and sometimes in fellowship with others he sought to evangelise while pursuing his daily employment. It was no surprise to anyone when a year or two after his marriage John sought commendation to a full-time service.

It was to Perthshire that John and Anna moved with that large county on their heart in 1967. Early on John acquired a little portable hall which he erected in various places around the district. Here, too, he came into contact with Jehovah's Witnesses on a scale he had never known in Ayrshire. Instead of ignoring them or condemning them as many are inclined to do, John has been very patient and studied their situation closely.

This booklet for Christian workers, who might contact J. W. 's, and its companion booklet for J. W. 's themselves are fruit of such study and contacts. Both are sent out with the prayer that such people, often disillusioned with empty religion previous to joining J. W.'s, might be led with your help to the knowledge and assurance of salvation.

A manual on counselling

JEHOVAH'S WITNESSES

Introduction ● The purpose of this booklet is to offer suggestions as to how Christians can be prepared to help those who are falsely called "Jehovah's Witnesses."

Such people for the most part have started as genuine seekers for truth and are more sinned against than sinning. The Watchtower Bible and Tract Society must accept responsibility for misguiding such people by their very deceptive form of propaganda. The mass-produced "Awake" and "Watchtower" Magazines provide the initial steps of this strategy. To follow up these a large quantity of books of varied titles do the damage of gradually brainwashing those who have been contacted, by a system of 'back calls' and 'Book Studies.' We have no hesitation in stating that those who teach the doctrines of this cult fall into the category described by the Lord Jesus in Matthew 15:14 as "blind leaders of the blind." Although they are devoutly religious, exceedingly zealous, and humanly intelligent, they are devoid of the Spirit of God and just as there were those in Israel

1

who "stumbled at the law" and had "corrupted the covenant" (Malachi 2:8) so the present-day Jehovah's Witness is guilty of wresting the scriptures (2 Peter 3:16).

Although the Jehovah's Witnesses will strongly resent the use of 2 Timothy 3:5-9 against them, it is a very apt description. The first feature is found in verse 6, Home Bible Studies, which in effect are really Book Studies. In verse 7 there is another feature, namely Studies, Lectures, constant learning, yet never arriving at the Truth. The reason why they are "never able to come to a knowledge of the truth" is that they are studying by the aid of the Watchtower CHANNEL of light which is presenting a biased slant on every verse of Scripture they ever read and as long as they persist they will be blind and their "sin remaineth"(John 9:41). Often Jehovah's Witnesses have challenged me and said, "If it is the Truth that you have why have I never come to interpret the Bible as you have? Why has God left me in the dark when all the time I have been searching for the Truth?" Quickly I have replied, "Because you are studying your Bible by the aid of the Watchtower books instead of by the aid of the Spirit of Truth (John 16:13; 1 Corinthians 2:9-16, verse 14 in particular). In point of fact it is your teacher who is wrong! You are seeking, ever learning, but you are consulting the wrong teacher. Your teacher should be God not man." He may retort that human teaching cannot be wrong because in Acts 8:31 the Ethiopian required someone to "guide him". True, but notice, as soon as the Ethiopian was brought to the point of understanding the way of salvation and was identified with Christ in baptism, v.39 says, "the

Lord caught away Philip." The Ethiopian was left without the human teacher. With an open Scripture and the Spirit of God to guide him as a believer, "he went on his way rejoicing." John says, "Ye need not that any man teach you, but the same anointing that ye have received, teacheth all things" (1 John 2:27). Thus soul winning amongst Jehovah's Witnesses involves acquainting yourself with their 'thought patterns' -how they have been trained to think and interpret the Bible's message.

The third feature mentioned in 2 Timothy 3 is found in verse 8, a dogmatic opposition to the true interpretation of scripture. With an air almost of spiritual arrogance they will stoutly resist the truth. They are convinced that no one can possibly refute their doctrinal position and when they see born again believers close their doors to them or refuse conversation they conclude it is because they are afraid or unable to defend what they believe. The result of this attitude is that it strengthens their faith in the Witness teaching instead of helping them to find a way out of the 'Religious Maze' to the light of personal salvation in Christ.

My Responsibility● What then must our attitude be to such people? Let me say here and now that I do not believe that 2 John 9-11 teaches that we should ignore them and refuse to present the Scriptures to them. Far too often I feel we use this Scripture as a convenient way out. I know the line of least resistance is the easiest, but it is not always the correct one. However, having stated this I now want to qualify a particular matter. If a young Christian, only recently saved, and not yet sufficiently grounded in the truth, were to engage in prolonged discussion with an experienced Jehovah's Witness, the outcome could be very unnerving. It would be wise to avoid this, as did the blind man of John 9:25, by giving a simple but convincing personal testimony of one's faith in Jesus Christ. Nevertheless, because of the large number who place themselves in this category, I want to give a challenge. Is it not true that many of us are sadly inexperienced in our understanding and defence of scriptural truth? Satan has done his work well and the propagandists of the Watchtower teaching are sometimes more capable of defending their "error" than some Christians are of defending the "Truth." Instead of turning tail every time, let us "search the Scriptures" in order to "earnestly contend for the faith" that we "may be able by sound doctrine both to exhort and convince the gainsayers" (Acts 17:11, Jude 3, Titus 1:9).

Let us never lose sight of the fact that Jehovah's Witnesses are nothing more and nothing less than poor lost sinners, and the Saviour who came to "seek that which was lost" (Luke 19:10) has commissioned us to do likewise and from that commission He has not eliminated Jehovah's Witnesses. We have no inhibitions about tackling other religious sects, oftentimes equally as false. Why therefore should we be less interested in winning the lost Jehovah's Witnesses? Is it because he has been indoctrinated better than some of the other cults? My first brush in earlier days with an experienced Watchtower pioneer just sent me to search deeper to find out really why I believed what I believed, an experience that would be worthwhile in the lives of

4

many Christians.

Face up to the fact that the winning of such people is not going to be easy. But also take encouragement from the fact that Jehovah's Witnesses are being set free from the bondage of Watchtower teaching and are finding true salvation in Christ, and not the Organization. Such information as this is not likely to create much impression upon a Jehovah's Witness as he will dismiss it lightly by quoting Acts 20:30 and 2 Thessalonians 2:3. However it should be of encouragement to us to know that such are not impossible cases. By observation I have noticed amongst those who have been saved and delivered from the organization that it has been a long process and this is understandable. One would not expect a person so deeply indoctrinated to relinquish his beliefs quickly. The normal process seems to be that gradual impressions are made over a prolonged period. It may have been through observing the consistent and godly life of a believer -someone outside of their Organization! Often the convincing presentation of Biblical Truth in a calm Christlike fashion has been used by the Holy Spirit to sow a seed into the mind and this has germinated after many days. When speaking to any contacts be prepared to be just a link in the chain of events that could result in that person's salvation. Remember your contribution could be for good or evil. You could help forward or you could repel by your attitude. May the Lord graciously show us the influence we can wield on people's lives.

Having, I trust, aroused each to their responsibilty in this matter, we now turn to consider some of the ways in which we can prepare to meet the need.

My Attitude ● Before considering any doctrinal matters, let me mention the importance of a correct attitude in one's person. While it is true that personalties never alter truth, nevertheless Jehovah's Witnesses are always very quick to judge one's teaching by the attitude shown in teaching. They will judge what you say by how you say it. It is extremely important for us to exercise caution and care when confronting such people with the Word of God. Avoid slighting or despising them. Show a genuine love for them, and interest in them. Never become spiteful even though their doctrines often degrade the Person of the Lord Jesus. Never become heated in discussion, and avoid any form of Scripture slinging. Be fully prepared to "reason with them out of the scriptures" (Acts 17:2) but avoid, as far as possible, all arguments which "gender strife" for "the servant of the Lord must not strive but be gentle unto all men, apt to teach, patient, in meekness instructing those that oppose themselves, if God peradventure will give them repentance to the acknowledging of the truth" (2Timothy 2:23-25)

While one does not advocate a study of all religious cults -the quantity of such and the time involved in studying all their doctrines would make such a proposition prohibitive -yet it is good to know where such go astray in order that a positive instruction may be given from the Word of God. If I wish to win an Arab to Christ I must learn his language, his culture, his thought patterns, and his beliefs. Similarly I suggest a measure of preparation to win the needy Jehovah's Witness. Having said this, let me say that the greatest preparation you can make is to saturate your mind with the truth of God. I believe the greatest asset to such militant sects is the sheer ignorance and unpreparedness of people who call themselves Christians! Be assured of this, most 'witnesses' will be fairly familiar with a good part of the Scriptures , especially such parts as may be twisted to suit their teaching. This, of course, is one of their basic failings -scripture is made to fit their doctrines, instead of their doctrine being shaped by Scripture.

Right with God ● In discussion you will be quickly challenged as to your attitude to blood transfusions, the celebration of Christmas, or military service. To the Jehovah's Witness these are some of the 'big' things! It is rather sad to think of how such basic matters as a righteous standing before God are relegated to something of secondary importance in comparision to such details. To say the least, it savours of the Pharisaical mistake of "omitting the weightier matters of the law". Matthew 23:23. He may try to justify his attitude by quoting Luke 16:10, "He that is faithful in that which is least is faithful also in much." Be ready however to show the real significance of this Scripture, "that which is least" is the stewardship of material possessions, "the mammon of unrighteousness," whereas "that which is much" is the stewardship of spiritual truth (1 Corinthians 4:1). It is therefore essential to turn the conversation to something of a more vital nature. Lift it to a higher plane.

Personal experience has taught the writer that the best subject on which to start conversation is not the deity of our Lord Jesus Christ, or the Trinity, or Christ's bodily resurrection, but the basis of one's salvation and righteousness with God. In the first place, this is the starting point for every sinner before he can understand the subsequent truths of holy scripture. God's desire as expressed in 1 Timothy 2:4 is to "have all men to be saved" (first), "and to come unto the knowledge of the truth" (second). Should we try to reverse the order? How can a person, devoid of spiritual life, and the capacity to receive spiritual truth, be expected to understand the revealed will of God? Secondly, it is just here that those who pride themselves as being rational and logical in their reasoning seem to fall down, as we shall observe in pursuing this point.

The normal atitude of the cultist is that salvation is something that one can never be "sure" of having received. Ask him if he has the assurance of personal salvation from sin. Ask him what he thinks will give him a righteous standing before God. Probably he will say something about keeping Jehovah's commands, or striving to follow Christ's teaching, or enduring to the end. First; be ready to explain the real meaning of Matthew 24:13. Show that it has nothing whatever to do with salvation from sin but physical salvation from bodily harm during "the great Tribulation" referred to in verse 21 onward. By presenting a convincing explanation from the actual context, you will have rocked his faith in what is a 'proof text' for the need of endurance before salvation can be received. Second, anticipate James 2. Your contact will be just waiting to jump in with this passage and therefore 'steal his thunder' by showing that you are perfectly familiar with this section of God's Word.

Show him that you agree entirely with James that "faith without works is dead." Once you have shown him that the "works" are not the ground or basis of salvation, but the evidence of genuine faith which has brought salvation, point out the significant words in verse 14 "though a MAN SAY he hath faith." The person of whom James is thinking is making only an outward profession of faith but is not genuine therefore "that (kind of) faith cannot save him." As with Matthew 7:21, a mere profession of Jesus as Lord is not enough. My life must give evidence of my faith. Genuine faith is backed up by works as a proof of salvation, but the foundation of salvation is still our faith in Christ as Saviour. At this point your contact will be trying to justify his position and will possibly endeavour to change his tactics and say that he also has faith in Christ. Therefore you must be ready with a third line of approach from the Scriptures to show how illogical his position really is.

In an unhurried way go over such scriptures as Ephesians 2:8-9, Romans 4:5: Romans 10:3. Press such passages home, ask him to read the words to you. Keep him to these until the Spirit of God has gripped him by a truth to which he has probably never before given thought. Turn him now to Romans 11:6 and show that like oil and water -grace and works will not mix together. If "works" play a part in obtaining the blessing of God, then all need for "grace" -God's undeserved kindness- is ruled out, by virtue of the fact that I will have earned it by personal merit. Back this up with Galatians 2:20, 21. Finally, from Romans 4;16 show how unreasonable his doctrinal position is. He claims to have "faith" yet has no "assurance." The reason why "the promise" can "be SURE" is because it is "of faith, by grace." Because salvation is by faith and not by works, it is possible to know, with utmost certainty, when one is saved. Read Philippians 4:3 and 1 John 5:13 to him. Clearly if he has no assurance of salvation this is evidence that he is not "trusting" in Christ by still "trying"-striving-keeping-enduring-working. Therefore he cannot know, and never will know, salvation or the assurance of it. One of the tricks of a Jehovah's Witness is to jump on to something else when he gets cornered but you must hold him to the passage. Don't argue, leave him with the Word. Allow the Holy Spirit to do a work of conviction

The Deity of Christ-Negative ● We now give consideration to the subject of the deity of our Lord Jesus Christ. Neither space nor time will allow for a lengthy treatise on this important subject. In view of the fact that complete volumes have been written on this subject, my remarks will be kept to a minimum. For a helpful work of a more exhaustive nature on Christ's deity, I recommend the reading of a small book "Jesus of Nazareth, who is He?" by Arthur Wallis.

I must remind you that members of the Jehovah's Witnesses are just as convinced against the deity of Christ as we would be for, and you will soon find them with no inhibitions against talking on this subject. In fact, they are so convinced by the Watchtower teaching on this matter that they honestly believe it is totally impossible to refute that viewpoint.

It is essential at the commencement of such a discussion to remind one concerning the inscrutability of the nature of God. "Canst thou by searching find out God? Canst thou find out the Almighty unto perfection?" (Job 11:7). With frail finite minds it is completely impossible for us to fully comprehend the Divine being. Your Witness friend will be waiting, of course, for you to say the doctrine of the Trinity is a 'mystery'-so avoid the trap and allow him no opportunity to pour scorn upon your belief in the absolute deity of the Lord Jesus Christ.

Frequently I find it helpful to dispose of their 'proof texts' first of all, lest having given an exposition of Christ's true nature and person, they endeavour to knock it all down again by quoting something which they believe supports their viewpoint. The most common text known and used in this connection by them is John 14:28, 'my Father is greater than I.' So let us start here. Note with him here that this is a glaring example of a text being taken from its context and thus becoming a pretext! Ask him why he did not quote the first word of the phrase, "for my Father is greater than I." The insertion of this little word makes all the difference to the meaning since it throws us back to the Lord's words in the first part of the verse. He had been intimating to His disciples the fact of His departure from them. Naturally they were sad at the news. The loss of the One who had companied with them for three and a half years would be painful. But says Christ, "If ye loved Me, ye would rejoice." Why?"For My Father is greater than I." What did Christ mean? Obviously He did not mean greater in His person but greater in His position. At that time Christ was "the Man of Sorrows and acquainted with grief." He was surrounded by hostile enemies who would cruelly entreat Him. The Father, however, was in a greater position, surrounded by holy angels-worshipped and served. Therefore, says Christ, you should not be sad but joyful at my going to such a position. If you really loved Me you would be glad to know of my going to the Father. Once in the presence of His Father Christ could never say, "My Father is greater than I." Notice Christ never taught, "My Father is BETTER than I." 'Better' is a term of comparision between natures (see Hebrews 1:4), while 'greater' is a term of comparison relative to positions.

Another favourite theme among Jehovah's Witnesses is Colossians 1:15, "the firstborn of every creature," and Revelation 3:14, "the beginning of the creation of God." Their conclusion from these statements is that Christ is a created being and thus inferior to the Father. How are we intended to understand the meaning? Let us deal with Colossians 1:15 first of all. It must be observed that the word "firstborn" is not necessarily a term of time but a term of rank and dignity. For proof of this examine (1)**Exodus 4:22**: "Israel is my son, even my firstborn." Obviously Israel was not the first nation in point of time. They at that time were surrounded by Egyptians-a nation much older than Israel. In what sense then was Israel God's firstborn? In no sense were they first in time but they were first in rank and dignity among the nations. (2)**Jeremiah 31:9**: "I am a father to Israel and Ephraim is my firstborn." Once more we

12

must observe the absence of the time factor. Ephraim was neither the first of Joseph's sons, nor did Israel come from the first of Jacob's sons. Again the term "firstborn" points to Ephraim's supremacy over the other tribes. (3)**Psalm 89:27:** Concerning David, who is referred to in verse 20, God says, "I will make him my firstborn, higher than the kings of the earth." We know from 1 Samuel 16:10-11 that David was the eighth and last of Jesse's sons, yet God refers to him as "my firstborn". As in the two preceding references, "firstborn" must of necessity refer to rank and dignity, and does not involve the time factor at all. Thus in the very same way, when we find Christ in Colossians 1:15 referred to as "the firstborn of every creature," it does not mean that He was the first created being, but points to His rank and dignity, His supremacy over creation. Why? Because as the following verse 16 shows, He is Creation's Creator, "Firstborn of every creature **for** by

Him were all things created." This statement is supported by John 1:3, and Hebrews 1:2.

From Colossians 4:16 we understand that the content and teaching of the Colossian epistle would be familiar to the church at Laodicea. It is not surprising then ,that in addressing that very church in Revelation 3:14, the Lord describes Himself as "the beginning of the Creation of God." Their familiarity with Colossians 1:15-16 would give them clear understanding that this further statement did not imply what the Witnesses teach that Christ was a created being.

In order to comprehend Revelation 3:14 aright we must

remember that in the book of Revelation the word "beginning" does not mean start but origin. For example, the very same word is used of God in Revelation 21:6, "the beginning and the end." This, even a Witness will agree, does not imply that there was a time when God started to exist or a time when He will cease to exist. Rather does it signify that God is the originator and consummator of all things. The same word is used of the Lord Jesus in Revelation 1:8 and 22:13. Thus in Revelation 3:14, "the beginning of the Creation of God" does not mean that Christ was the start of all that God created, but that He Himself is the all-glorious origin of the entire creation.

Many of the Jehovah's Witnesses find a problem in 1 Corinthians 11:3, "the head of Christ is God." Therefore be prepared to give the true sense of the passage. It is dealing with headship, and headship does not imply superiority as the preceding phrase would make clear, "the head of the woman is the man." This surely does not imply that women are inferior human beings or men superior, but that the Divine order is that women have a place of subjection as is also true with regard to Christ in the Godhead. There is no thought of inferiority as to His person. He is every bit as much God as is the Father, just as the woman is every bit as human as is the man. Headship does not imply superiority, nor does subordination imply inferiority, either in the human or the Divine realm. The parallel passage of 1 Corinthians 15:27-28 must be viewed in a similiar way. The voluntary subjection of the Son is not that the Father may be all in all, but that God in all His fulness, Father, Son, and Holy Spirit, may be all in all.

14

One other passage that is liable to be raised is 1 Corinthians 8:6, "But to us there is but one God, the Father, of whom are all things and we in Him, and one Lord Jesus Christ by whom are all things and we by Him." To a Jehovah's Witness this means that only the Father is God and the Lord Jesus is inferior. However the context reveals the true interpretation. In verse 5 Paul is thinking of the realm of heathendom with their gods many, and lords many, but in verse 6 to us there is only one God -one Lord. But why the distinction between "God" and "Lord"? A "god" is an object of worship -a "lord" is one to whom undivided allegiance is given, one who authoritatively guides the service of his devotees. We have One who is the object of our worship, and One who authoritatively controls our service. But we are not to understand for one moment that the Father -the object of our worship, is superior to Jesus Christ -the Lord who directs our service. If the argument is put forward from this verse that it would be wrong to call Jesus Christ "God", one must logically conclude that it would be also wrong to call the Father "Lord". But this is totally impossible as there are many scriptures which refer to the Father as "Lord", for example, Luke 2:26, "the Lord's Christ," which the Jehovah's Witness own New World Translation translates as "the Christ of Jehovah." This verse does not eliminate the Father from being called "Lord." Therefore it does not eliminate the Son from being called "God" either. With this John 20:28 agrees, where Thomas acknowledges Jesus as both "Lord" and "God."

Having cornered your opponent, he will be quickly

15

thinking of a way out. His years of 'brain-washing' will not permit him to accept the evidence of Scripture easily, therefore he will look for a 'loop-hole ' in a passage such as Isaiah 9:6. He thinks such a verse will throw "light" on the difficulty. He will explain that Christ is "a" god -yes, even "the Mighty God," but he will quickly add "not the Almighty." He will tell you that Satan is called "a" god also, "the god of this world" (2 Corinthians 4:4). In reply, show that the term, "the Mighty God" applies not merely to Christ, but the very next chapter (Isaiah 10:21) speaks of Israel's God as "the Mighty God." Ask him to read to you Jeremiah 32:18 from his own translation. This reference shows that "the Mighty God" is Jehovah of hosts Himself. Such evidence is rather unnerving to a Witness! Further endeavour to show that Christ is "the Almighty" by using the following Scriptures.

Revelation 1:17, 18 describes "the first and the last" as the One who "liveth and was dead" -a clear reference to the Lord Jesus. Although chapter 21:6 describes God as "the Alpha and the Omega," chapter 22:12, 13 uses the same title of the Lord Jesus. The usage of the New World Translation can be useful here as it puts verses 12-15 in inverted commas as being the language of the One who is coming quickly. So the Lord Jesus is "the Alpha and the Omega, the beginning and the end, the first and the last." Turn back after proving this point to examine chapter 1:8. The same One who is the first and the last, "the Alpha and the Omega," is "the Almighty."! The "Mighty God" of Isaiah 9:6 is therefore "the Almighty." If they persist and say there must be more than one who is "the first and last," show them

Isaiah 44:6 where "Jehovah of Hosts" says," I am the first and I am the last and beside me there is no God."

The Deity of Christ-Positive ● Earlier I stated that this booklet was not intended to be an exhaustive work on the deity of Christ. Allow me, however, to pursue one further line of thought, by way of positive suggestion. So far much that I have said on this subject has been of a defensive nature, Let me now give something of an offensive nature. I am being deliberately selective. Many scriptures might be cited but I avoid any which a Jehovah's Witness may endeavour to discredit.

Frequently I find it extremely helpful to consider a passage such as John 5:17-23. By using such, you are able to give the sense from the entire context, and therefore avoid giving the impression that you base your belief on a few obscure and isolated texts of scripture

Observe the background. Christ is being criticised, not merely because of His healing on the sabbath, but because of His claim that God was His Father (verse 18). Christ knew that Jewish thought would conclude from His personal claim that He was equal with God. Christ knew that to a Jewish mind a claim to sonship implied a claim to equality with the Father. A Jehovah's Witness will quickly point out that it was the Jews, not Christ, who said He was "equal with God." Admittedly, but Christ **knew** that they would interpret His own claim

17

in this very way. If Christ is not "equal with God" then He must be guilty of two things. (1) The sin of Lucifer, who in Isaiah 14:14 said, "I will be like the Most High." (2) He is also guilty of completely misleading and utterly deceiving those to whom He spoke, for He makes a bold statement knowing completely how Jewish minds would react -causing them to make a statement which Jehovah's Witnesses believe is unscriptural and blasphemous. Knowing the character of our Lord Jesus Christ, if they had misunderstood His personal claim, He would surely have corrected it there and then. How did Paul react in Acts 14:15, and Peter in Acts 10:26, and the angel in Revelation 19:10; 22:9? Surely if such inferior beings acted in such a becoming way, it is unthinkable that our Lord Jesus Christ would allow this matter to pass, if it was a case of error and misunderstanding. Without doubt we are driven conclusively to the viewpoint that the reason why Jesus Christ did not contradict the statement made by the Jews was because He was "equal with God."

This is further substantiated by observing the teaching that Christ goes on to give. In actual fact, He now proves that their own conclusion is exactly true! He is "equal with God"! It is as though Christ was saying to the Jews, "You haven't misunderstood my claim in verse 17 -you are right enough, I am equal with God."

In verses 19-20 He shows He is "equal" in the performing of His Works. The Son will never act independently of the Father (verse 19), but in verse 20, the other side of the coin, the Father will never act independently of the Son. He "sheweth Him all things that

Himself doeth." These verses teach that what one does, the other does "likewise" -equality in working.

In verse 21, He shows he is "equal" in His power to raise the dead. Moses in Deuteronomy 32:39, Hannah in 1 Samuel 2:6, and David in Psalm 68:20 all recognize that God (Jehovah) alone has the power to raise dead ones. Here the Lord Jesus claims the same power.

In verse 23 He shows He is "equal" in His position of honour. This is one of the most staggering claims ever made by our Lord Jesus. Imagine these words on the lips of anyone else, for example Paul the apostle, or even Michael the archangel! What blasphemy! Christ here demands the honour, worship, reverence, that has to be given to the Father. I say again, what preposterous blasphemy if Christ be not "equal with God"! In Acts 12:22, 23 Herod was smitten in judgement because he accepted the worship that should have been given to God, yet Christ here is demanding it, not merely accepting it. The obligation to "honour the Son" is just as important as the obligation to "honour the Father." Ask your Jehovah's Witness friend if he honours Christ this way ? He will claim to honour the Son but note the words "even as," New World Translation "just as." That is, one must not be worshipped as superior to the other. Hold him to these words -they are damaging and devastating to the complete Watchtower heresy of Arianism. In Matthew 4:10 the Lord Jesus said, "Thou shalt worship the Lord thy God and Him only shalt thou serve." Scripture teaches that any other worship is idolatry, yet here Christ demands the same worship as the Father and in Hebrews 1:6 the Father commands, "Let all the angels of God worship Him" -the Son. Once more we are driven to acknowledge that Christ must be "equal with God."

In concluding my remarks on the deity of Christ, let me just cite a few helpful scriptures with the briefest of comment.

Colossians 2:9. "In Him dwelleth all the fulness of the Godhead bodily." The word for Godhead is 'theotetos,' the genitive of theotes,' which actually means 'divinity' or 'deity,' and not "divine quality," as the New World Translation translates it. Divine quality is expressed in the Greek by "theotes" (Romans 1:20).

A simple comparison between Isaiah 6:1-10 and John 12:39-41 will show that Jehovah, whom Isaiah saw, verse 5, was actually the Lord Jesus, for it was actually He of whom he spoke -John 12:41. Although the Jehovah's Witness translation alters Hebrews 1:8 to read in a clumsy, almost unintelligible way, the evidence is fairly obvious that the Father is addressing the Son, and in doing so, calls Him "God". We might add, if anyone knows rightly who the Son is surely it is the Father!

The Doctrine of the Trinity ● We admit that the teaching of three persons in one Godhead is not easily understood, and even less easily proved by logic. I remind you however of my remarks earlier, on the inscrutability of God, and would warn of the dangers of confining God to the narrow limits of our small minds. It is easy to sin like the people in Psalm 50:21 to whom God said, "Thou thoughtest I was altogether such an one as thyself," or like those in Romans 1:23, "who changed the glory of the incorruptible God into an image" -something to fit the scope of their finite minds. We must remind all Watchtower followers that this is wrong and cannot be done without violating the scriptures.

We know the word "Trinity" never occurs in the Bible, but then neither do some of the words that they use, such as "theocracy". What really matters is that the truth of the three persons in one Godhead does occur in the Scriptures. Take time to explain what we really believe the Trinity is -three distinctive persons in one Godhead. Sometimes they put it over as though Christians believe in three Gods, or just one person, and thus they talk disparagingly about a three-headed God. It is essential to clear the decks and present what orthodox really does teach.

To help understand the problem of three persons yet one God, I sometimes quote the parallel idea as presented in Genesis 2:24 and Ephesians 5:31. "Therefore shall a man leave his father and his mother and cleave unto his wife, and they shall be one flesh." No one could conclude from this that the man and woman are not two distinct persons. Two persons yet "one" flesh. So with regard to the Trinity.

The Father is called "God" 1 Corinthians 8:6; 1 Peter 1:2.

The Son is called "God" Romans 9:5; Titus 2:13; Hebrews 1:8.
The Holy Spirit is called "God" Acts 5:3,4 : compare 2 Corinthians 3:18.

Additional evidence of the Triune nature of the Godhead is seen in the wording of the baptismal formula of Matthew 28:19, "Name of the Father, and of the Son, and of the Holy Ghost." Compare 2 Corinthians 13:14; Ephesians 4: 4-6; Corinthians 12:5-9.

This is further corroborated by the usage of the plural, for example, Genesis 1:26, "Let US make man in OUR image," yet in the following verse "God created man in His (own) image." Such a passage rules out completely the possibility of God being a single Person as Jehovah's Witnesses teach.

Thus when we read in John 10:30, "I and my Father are one," this is not the oneness of will and design merely, but as the context shows, oneness of power and operation. Jehovah's Witnesses err in comparing this with the oneness of John 17:20-22. In John 10 the context shows that Christ was claiming, not merely the same will and purpose as the Father, but the same irresistible power as the Father: "Neither shall any man pluck them out of my hand"(verse 28), "no man is able to pluck them out of my Father's hand" (verse 29). The Lord ascribes the same thing to Himself as to the Father. He promises eternal security to His followers, because of His and the Father's Almighty power. The response of the Jews in verse 31 shows how they had interpreted, "I and My Father are one." They obviously deduced that He meant oneness of essence, equality, and godhead, and therefore sought to stone Him. Had the Jews received a false impression, He would undoubtedly have corrected this, but rather than do that Christ makes further statements to confirm that He was One in essence with the Father, with the result that in verse 39 they still seek His life.

The Resurrection of Christ ● We now offer a few suggestions on the scriptural viewpoint of the resurrection of Jesus Christ. Frequently I find this a very profitable subject on which to converse with Jehovah's Witnesses. Their teaching is that Christ did not rise bodily but that He rose as a 'mighty spirit creature' -His body being either dissolved in gases, or like that of Moses, laid up as a grand memorial of God's love!

The two principal scriptures upon which they base this teaching are 1 Corinthians 15:45, "the last Adam was made a quickening spirit," and 1 Peter 3:18, "made alive in spirit" (literal Greek). First then let us examine these.

1 Corinthians 15:45 is not referring to the bodily form of Christ or Adam but to the kind of life within them. "The first Adam was made a living soul," means Adam had 'soul life,' or life of the natural man. Christ as a "life-giving spirit" had spiritual life or life fitted for Heaven. Hence this passage contextually cannot be interpreted to mean that Christ was raised as a "spirit."

There is every evidence that "the Spirit" referred to in

1 Peter 3:18 is the Holy Spirit Himself. The verse is in perfect harmony with Romans 8:11, "the Spirit of Him that raised up Jesus from the dead," indicating that when Christ was "made alive in spirit" he was made alive in the power of the Holy Spirit. Thus these main objections raised by Witnesses against the bodily resurrection are all answered by the Scriptures themselves, and constitute no threat to the historic Christian doctrine of the resurrection.

The fact of Christ's bodily resurrection is foundational to all of the Christian faith. 1 Corinthians 15 states five dreadful results if the resurrection is not true.

1. v. 14. The apostles' preaching is vain-devoid of substance.
2. vv. 14, 17. The faith of believers is vain -pointless.
3. v. 15. The apostles, God's true witnesses, are liars-in point of fact it is Jehovah's Witnesses who are the liars.
4. v. 17. There is no possibility of salvation-nothing to blot out our sin, or bring "justification," See Romans 4:25.
5. v. 18. All our loved ones have perished-death would not be "gain" (Philippians 1:21).

Surely we rejoice in the words of the apostle, "But now is Christ risen from the dead" (verse 20). The actual literal resurrection of Jesus Christ is a vital and integral part of the plan of salvation. This is completely taken from us if we suggest that it was merely a 'spiritual resurrection.' The whole weight of evidence of New Testament teaching is that the One who died and was

24

buried has been raised from the dead. On various occasions Christ deliberately ate and drank to prove to His disciples that He was physically alive from the dead-Luke 24:41-43; John 21:12-14; Acts 10:41. Jehovah's Witnesses endeavour to explain this matter by suggesting that Christ must have assumed a body of a material form for a limited period just to encourage the faith of the disciples. This is a dreadful perversion on two scores. One, no such thing is even hinted at in the Scriptures, and two, it savours of complete fraud. To take a body in order to prove something which is not true, is deception! Surely the reason why Christ did eat and drink was to prove to the disciples the reality of His resurrection. He was not merely spiritually, but literally alive.

There is scriptural evidence that Christ did rise bodily-in a glorified form of the actual body which He possessed before His death. Speaking to the unbelieving Jews in John 2 Christ said, "Destroy this temple and in three days I will raise it up" (verse 19).

The Jews misunderstood His meaning and misinterpreted his words as referring to the temple in Jerusalem. However, the apostle John clearly explains the Lord's meaning: "But He spake of the temple of His body" (verse 21).

The very body put to death-"it" would be raised up again. Such a passage is inescapable evidence of the bodily resurrection of Christ. Further, the words of Luke 24:37-40 are valuable evidence: "a spirit hath not flesh and bones as ye see me have" (verse 39).

It is clearly unthinkable that Christ would materialize a body on this occasion (as Jehovah's Witnesses teach), in order to "prove" He was not a spirit, yet all the time, according to the Witnesses, He was a spirit! Not only did the Lord have "flesh and bones," but "hands and feet" (verse 40), which bore the wounds of Calvary. These were offered as tangible evidence of His bodily resurrection.

In John 20 the body in which He showed Himself alive to Thomas was obviously the same body in which He died at Calvary. Observe the words, "Reach hither thy finger and behold my hands? reach hither thy hand, and thrust it into My side" (verse 27). The only way to reject is to wilfully deny the Bible.

In Mark 16:6 the angel presented the absence of Jesus' body as a proof of His resurrection, "He is risen, He is not here." If the body of the Lord Jesus was not resurrected, as the Witnesses teach, the absence of the body actually proved nothing! The angel either was deluded or presented false evidence!

You will probably find that somewhere through a discussion on the resurrection, a Witness will raise the point that bodily resurrection is impossible, as this would cancel out the ransoming of the human race. This sounded very strange the first time I heard it, and therefore it is wise to be prepared for this point. Although they offer no scripture to support the view, they believe it was His human life which He offered as a ransom and therefore He could not take it back. To counter this strange doctrine, make a comparison between Matthew 20:28, "the Son of man came . . . to give His life (psuche) a ransom for many," and John 10:17, 18, ". . . I lay down my life (psuche) that I may take it again" . . . "I have power to lay IT down, and I have power to take IT again." Clearly these scriptures show that what He laid down as "a ransom for many," He took again in resurrection.

One final word on this subject. Probably the greatest difficulty for a Witness, in accepting the bodily resurrection of Christ, is the fact that some of those who knew Him best in life apparently did not recognize Him in resurrection. The three major scriptures they cite are (a) John 20:11-16 Mary in the garden. (b) Luke 24:13-35 The two disciples on the road to Emmaus. (c) John 21:4-14 the disciples on the shore.

There is however a perfectly natural explanation in each instance, and we need not be alarmed by the contention raised by Witnesses.

(a) **John 20:11-16**
E. Gruss in his excellent book "Apostles of Denial" (pp. 137-139) gives seven reasons why Mary did
not recognize the Lord Jesus. I here cite in brief. (1) John 20:1 says, "It was yet dark" when Mary came to the sepulchre. Her failure to recognize Christ could have been caused by the darkness. (2) Mary's thoughts are shown to be occupied completely with grief. Mary was neither startled on seeing the angels, nor did she address them.

The word used for Mary's weeping is 'klaio,' which means loud and unrestrained weeping. Her eyes were blurred with tears when she saw Jesus. (3) v. 14 says that Mary turned toward Christ, and again in verse 16 she turned toward Him. The second use of 'turn' seems to imply that she had not looked fully at Him before. (4) One must not overlook the fact of Christ's cloth-ing being different. (5) Mary was not looking for the risen Christ. Her mind was far from an ac-complished resurrection. (6) Orthodoxy does not believe that Christ looked exactly the same as before His death. Christ was no longer the Man of Sorrows; His face reflected the glory and triumph of His resurrection. (7) It is only natural that Mary would turn and recognize Christ when He spoke her name. She was a stranger there, and hearing her name opened her eyes to recog-nize Him.

(b)   **Luke 24: 13-35**
The reason why these two disciples did not rec-ognize Christ is actually stated in the pas-sage. In verse 16 we read, "Their eyes were holden that they should not know him." The language used designates a power outwith th-emselves: they were kept from recognizing Him until verse 31, when "their eyes were opened and they knew Him." Christ was deliberately keeping His iden-tity hidden for the moment. Actually, the pas-sage suggests that Christ was so easily recog-nized that it required a deliberate hiding, to keep him from being recognized right away. E. Gruss

also suggests other reasons why they did not recognize Him but does admit that these are unneccessary in view of the fact that the passage gives ample reason itself.

(c) **John 21: 4-14**

The reason for the non-recognition of Christ on the part of the disciples would again be best listed under three simple points: (1) These men had returned to their earthly calling and did not recognize Him because they were occupied with bodily needs. (2) They had been fishing during the 'night' (verse 3), and thus in the early morning light (verse 4) they did not quickly recognize Christ. (3) Add to the foregoing statements the fact that verse 8 says that they were about "two hundred cubits" -approximately 100 yards "from land." Is it surprising that they did not recognize the Lord?

As you will have deduced by now the Witnesses, on the subject of the resurrection of Christ, have very little convincing Scriptural support for their erroneous doctrine. If you can shake their confidence on a matter like this, they will begin to question what the Organization teaches. This is what you must aim at first, as they are absolutely convinced that it is a complete impossibilty for the Watchtower Organization to be doctrinally wrong! They will never listen to you teaching the Truth until first their confidence is shaken from that which is wrong. If the Organization is wrong on one point, possibly it could be wrong on other points! As one ex-Witness in his testimony states-you must knock one 'little brick' out of their system of thought.

**The New
World Translation** ● Before concluding this booklet, I must say just a little on the official translation of the Watchtower Society of Jehovah's Witnesses. It is called the New World Translation (N.W.T.). Although a great deal could be said with regard to this version, or "perversion,' I confine my remarks to the minimum of details.

Although the translators claim consistency, they apparently violate their own claims whenever the occasion demands this to give weight to their own particular doctrinal viewpoint. Two examples must suffice.

1. **The use of the Greek word "Kurios" (Lord),** which the New World translators have changed to "Jehovah." For example, see Romans 10. Verse 13 they translate as follows: "Everyone who calls on the name of Jehovah (kurios) will be saved." However, in verse 9 of the same passage, they translate, "For if you publicly declare that word in your own mouth, that Jesus is Lord (kurios). . . you will be saved." Why is "kurios" translated "Jehovah" in one verse yet in the other left unaltered as "Lord"? There is only one answer. Consistence of translation would have demanded a confession of Jesus as "Jehovah," but this would cut across Watchtower teaching, so the translation is made to fit!

The same thing is seen in Romans 14. In verse 8 three times over "kurios" is translated Jehovah, yet in verse 9 "kurios" is translated "Lord." To do otherwise, of course, would be to teach that "Christ-is Jehovah both of the dead and the living." But as Jehovah's Witnesses don't believe that, the preconceived doctrine determines the translation.

2.The use of the Greek word"proskuneo" (Worship)
In John 4:20-24, the word is used ten times and each time both in the Authorised Version and the New World Translation it is translated "worship." For example, "The Father seeketh such to worship Him" (verse 23). However, when we turn to passages relating to the person of the Lord Jesus, we find that the New World Translation changes the very same word to "obeisance." For example Luke 24:52, "they did obeisance to Him." Compare Matthew 2:11; Matthew 8:2; Matthew 9:18; John 9:38; Matthew 20:20; Matthew 28:9, 17.

Actually, the "worship" which the disciples gave to Christ in Matthew 14:33 was because they saw Him in verses 25-32 do what only God the Creator can do (See Job 9:8; Psalm 77:19)-tread upon the waves of the sea and still the tempest. Therefore they worshipped Christ as God Himself. It is very obvious that the translators have been anxious to preserve their doctrinal teaching on the inferiority of Christ by seeking to ascribe "worship" to the Father, but "obeisance" to the Son-despite the undisputed fact of it being the selfsame word in the Greek. Surely all of this savours of tragic doctrinal bias which is more careful to preserve the soceity's teaching than to give accurate translation of scripture. Such a version must be shown to be unworthy of one's confidence.

My Equipment ● In conclusion, I suggest that every Christian should be equipped, not only with a working knowledge of Bible doctrine, but also with good helpful literature to distribute to Witnesses. They proselytise themselves by means of the printed page, and we also should make capital of such means of propagating the Word of God. This booklet is written particularly for Christians to offer practical help and teaching in confronting the Witnesses, but the need for a booklet for mass distribution to the Witnesses has prompted the present writer ro produce one entitled, "Why Christians cannot accept Jehovah's Witness teaching." It contains much of the material contained in this counselling manual, but is intended for distribution.

Much literature has been written in condemnation of the Witness standpoint, but a great deal of this is totally unsuitable for giving to the Witnesses. Some of it actually has done the cause of Christianity more harm than good and has given occasion to the "enemies of the Lord to blaspheme." We must exercise extreme caution and be very selective in the material used. I suggest the following literature from personal experience as helpful:

(a) "Apostles of Denial" by Edmond Charles Gruss (Presbyterian and Reformed Publishing Co.)-324 pages.

Especially for the student and person who is regularly contacting Jehovah's Witnesses. This is a standard work on the history, doctrines, and claims of the cult.

(b) "We left Jehovah's Witnesses," by Edmond Charles Gruss (Baker Book House, Grand Rapids, Michigan)-169 pages. A very readable book presenting the personal testimony of a number of people from different backgrounds who have broken completely with the society. They have left, not over personal grievance, but on account of doctrinal conflict. The challenge of salvation also comes over in this book.

(c) "Jesus of Nazareth-who is He?" by Arthur Wallis (C.L.C. London)-55 pages. This book deals exclusively with the deity of Christ. It is a decidely helpful publication, which, with confidence, you could leave with a Witness. Whilst written for Jehovah's Witnesses, it virtually never mentions them.

(d) "Jehovah's Witnesses-Their Translation" by Henry J. Heydt (American Board of Missions to the Jews, Inc. Box 1331 Englewood Cliffs, N.J. 07632)-19 pages. A small booklet with a real challenge. It is very damaging to the Watchtower cause, exposing their translation as a biased travesty of God's Holy Word.

(e) "Jehovah's Witnesses and the Deity of Jesus Christ." "Jehovah's Witnesses and the Resurrection of Jesus Christ." By Walter R. Martin (Evangelical Tract Distributors, PO Box 146 Edmonton Alta Canada

T5J 2G9)-these are two separate small leaflets which, though brief, have a definite challenging message and are excellent for mass distribution.

One final suggestion. One of the weaknesses of people who have become Jehovah's Witnesses is that they are susceptible to book studies. That is how the Organization probably caught them to begin with. It is therefore possible, in some cases, still to use this method. Leave a copy of one of the above listed books. Arrange to call back after say two weeks. Take another copy of the same book, and, depending on the length of this book, read either part or all of the book to the person concerned. Underline various points and turn to the Scripture references given as you proceed. Let the Word of God speak and the Spirit of God work. Close the visit with a brief word of prayer. Thank the Witness for listening and, if possible, leave another book and arrange to call in another two weeks for another 'Bible Study.' Maintain a spirit of calm Christlike courage, trusting that "God peradventure will give them repentance to the acknowledging of the truth."

GW00597401

'Chatting over hot chocolate with my book agent one rainy day, she asked me about my outfit. I began to gush as I relayed the story of finding it at a flea market in Manhattan. She stopped me in my tracks and said: "That's it! That's what you need to write about."'

Lynne McCrossan lives in Edinburgh and shops all over the UK. Style Columnist for the *Edinburgh Evening News*, Style Expert on STV's *The Hour* and a Contributor Fashion Expert on BBC Radio Scotland, Lynne's career has spanned print, radio and TV, including being Host of TV show *The Hirer*. This is her first book.

A Girl's Guide to

Vintage

LYNNE McCROSSAN

Luath Press Limited

EDINBURGH

www.luath.co.uk

First published 2010

ISBN: 978-1-906817-46-6

The paper used in this book is recyclable.
It is elemental chlorine free (ECF)
and manufactured from sustainable
wood pulp forests. This paper and
its manufacture are approved by the
National Association of Paper Merchants
(NAPM), working towards a more
sustainable future.

Printed and bound by
Thomson Litho, East Kilbride

Typeset in Quadraat & FS Albert by
3btype.com

Look Book photographs of Zoe Hill
© Brian Sweeney;
Look Book photographs of Lynne
McCrossan © Greg Macvean;
photograph on page 35 by Artpunk.

Contents

A Girl's Thank You...

To the man who held my hand, wiped my tears, booted my bum, fed me chicken, made me giggle but best of all still stands beside me when any sane person would have bolted. I love you.

To all the wonderful women in my life, Kathryn, Steph, Auntie Em and Bunty.

Mum, you taught me everything I know, it's a pity I'm still rubbish with money! You are my best friend and I thank the universe everyday that you're my muma.

My girls (Guffball, Quinn and Lou), you are more than my best friends, you are my sisters. I'd be blessed to have one friendship like ours, to land three makes me incredibly lucky.

Gwen, thank you doesn't cut it. You are the love of my life.

Swedo, how you got what was in my head onto those pages still astounds me. You are a beautiful man, and you know it.

To my personal pap Greg, thank you for being my mirror... X

Zobo, you are my creative driving force. We'll always be 16 in my head. I love that the year my book was born you became a mother – I am so proud of you.

My Luath Press Lovelies (Leila, Christine, Jo, Lesley, Chani and Sarah) without you there would be no book. I am honoured to call you my girlfriends.

Senga, you are a super woman. I don't know how you created such beauty – thank you.

Jenny Brown, thank you for giving me this idea and helping push everything through.

To Aileen Harris and Iain Allardyce, and Joanne Cruickshank, Fraser Leslie and Zara Knott, for coming to our aid at the last minute with photos for Cardiff and Aberdeen.

To all the fabulous vintage stores, their owners and every contributor, you made this process so fun.

East Coast Trains, Virgin Trains, First Scotrail, Stenaline, Southern Trains, The Hempel Hotel, My Hotel Chelsea, Visit Cardiff – I am eternally grateful for your goodwill.

To Pop... X

A Girl's *Introduction*

It was December 2008, I was 24, and reeling from being made redundant not once but twice by the same employer in the space of nine short months. I had been working at a radio station in Edinburgh, a job I had fought for tooth and nail. But on the night before Christmas, I found myself saying goodbye to the people I'd spent every waking moment with for the previous three years. Little did I suspect that losing my job would have such a deep, psychological impact, comparable to losing my father a decade before. I had no choice in either of those episodes and, at that point, the way forward was lost to me.

As the weeks merged into one another, I found solace and escapism in what had always been my favourite pastime – browsing through second-hand stores. You see, whenever I need to focus and clear my thoughts, there is only one thing that fits the bill. Vintage shopping. For as far back as my memory allows, I have been fascinated by all things old. My grandfather, historic buildings, classic movies and timeless music, but clothes – their texture, their smell, their story – knock all of that into a cocked hat.

My moment of clarity came quite unexpectedly. A girlfriend was looking for a special dress, a one-of-a-kind that wouldn't break the bank. Naturally, I took her vintage shopping. It was only then I realised what I needed to be doing with my life had been right underneath my nose all this time. My enduring love affair with clothes from other eras, my determination never be caught wearing the same thing as anyone else, and my uncanny knack for bargain hunting, itself inherited from a ferociously frugal mother, were paraphernalia I should be passing on.

So this is my gift to you. I'm sharing my favourite vintage haunts and will show you how embracing the old can transform your shopping habits and wardrobe, with stylish, unconventional, recession-friendly fashion.

A Girl's Guide to *Edinburgh*

Edinburgh is the grandaddy of vintage. The whole place reeks of the past. You'll find medieval, Georgian, Victorian and modern structures nestling in close proximity, and shopping for vintage in the city reflects that.

This is the place I've called home since I was 17 and the shops I'm about to share with you are some of my most treasured. Edinburgh is relatively small, so there is no reason why you can't stroll from one store to another, soaking up the sites. What are we waiting for? Let's go vintage shopping!

The Trinity

Everyone has their favourite shop. I like to think of them as 'go to' places. For some it's Armani, for others it's Primark. Regardless, it's the place you know will never let you down. That familiar feeling consumes you as soon as you walk through the door, autopilot takes over, and before you know it, your card has been accepted and that hit stays with you for the rest of the day.

Of course, my vintage weakness evolved when Madonna was still Like A Virgin, so it won't surprise you to know that my 'go to' place morphed into three 'go to' places long ago. I call them The Holy Trinity: in the name of the Father (Herman Brown); the Son (Godiva); and the Holy Spirit (Armstrong's). Amen. When you come to my nation's capital, go native. Do the tourist trail, by all means, but what I'm about to divulge will let you have your cake and eat it too: sight-seeing and vintage combined.

Look out for: The antique wedding dresses.

Prices: Anna understands that vintage needs to feel like a bargain. Her pricing is very reasonable – dresses range from £20 to £60 on average. Really special items are considerably more.

Herman Brown · 151 WEST PORT · EDINBURGH · EH3 9DP · 0131 228 2589

www.hermanbrown.co.uk

Let's start off at the top of West Port, affectionately dubbed the 'pubic triangle' because of certain gentlemen's establishments. Here you will find the Father, Herman Brown. Its dark wooden floors, sash windows and high ceilings give the feeling of stepping into someone's very elaborate dressing room. Every item is lovingly picked by the owner. Beautiful dresses taunt you from the walls, just daring you to try them on. The railings are sensibly split from tops to dresses, suits to coats. The shoes and belts sit beside the cash desk, which itself straddles a Pandora's box of costume jewellery, a glass treasure trove that's stolen many hours of my time. On the tables in the middle of the room you can rummage through scarves and hats to your heart's content, but the unmissable focal point is the bust, a chameleon-like display that appears to change more often than my underwear. Right at the back lurks a Wham! lamp circa 1983. There's no point haggling – it's not for sale – but it lends itself to the unique atmosphere.

The icing on Herman Brown's cake is Anna Nicolson, the store's owner. She opened HB in 1984, selling second-hand clothes simply because new stock at that time was too expensive for her to buy. Her quality control is exceptional, with clothes from the '20s right through to the early '90s, all in impeccable condition.

Look out for: The extensive selection of knitwear.

Prices: Godiva's vintage is affordable, around £30 a dress.

12

Godiva 9 WEST PORT · EDINBURGH · EH1 2JA · 0131 221 9212

www.godivaboutique.co.uk

From HB we head 100 yards down the hill towards the Son, Godiva.
The newest kid on the block sits on a narrow street at the foot of the
Grassmarket, and it's the edgiest way to shop for vintage in Edinburgh.
The current owner started off as a Saturday girl in the original premises
while she was a student. Fleur McIntosh bought the boutique and moved it
to a different location, where she has managed to stamp her own twist on
the store. When you first arrive you get that 'kid in a candy store' feeling.
Everything is heavenly, from the Victorian cornicing to the gilded mirrors,
not to mention the clothes.

Godiva is set up in two
parts. I like to think of
these as the Old Town
and the New Town,
just like our city.
New designers from
Edinburgh College of Art take centre
stage, while old fabrics are reworked
for one-off pieces. There's also the
option of having a dress custom made.
It's the back of the shop that really
excites me, though. Wander through to
find old clothes painstakingly repaired
or altered, each with a tag telling you
a little more about their history. The
majority of Fleur's stock comes from
Europe, so there's a crazy mix of styles
and decades to choose from. It's like
speed dating for vintage lovers. Ms
McIntosh's attention to detail makes
shopping in Godiva unbeatable.

Strangely, I can't remember a time
when it wasn't there, a bit like the
Victorian fireplace in her back room.

Look out for: The fabulous prom dresses.

Prices: In my experience, Armstrong's is by far the priciest way to shop for vintage in Edinburgh, but you can't put a price on love. And there's always the option of bartering with whoever is serving. On average, dresses start around £40.

Armstrong's
81-83 GRASSMARKET · EDINBURGH · EH1 2HJ · 0131 220 5557
www.armstrongsvintage.co.uk

Last but not least in my Trinity is The Holy Spirit. Armstrong's. The shop is an institution in Edinburgh, and its family of owners are steeped in the history of the rag and bone trade. The flagship store has treats and surprises that will keep you captivated and coming back for more. There's a second Armstrong's on South Clerk Street, as well as another little gem on Teviot Place formerly known The Rusty Zip, but there's something so special about the Grassmarket store that it makes me tingle every time. Once inside, I regress back to a small child in awe of my surroundings. There's an *Alice In Wonderland* charm to it of pure fantasy, decadence and excess. It's an assault on the senses. That unmistakable second-hand smell of the past just clobbers you, with garments crammed into every available crevice.

What sets this shop apart from any other is that it could be mistaken for a clothes museum. A small number of items are on a strictly 'look only' basis – but feel free to get your hands dirty elsewhere. Armstrong's vast collection may seem a little daunting to the uninitiated – so be prepared to dig deep and push your way through the decades.

Night

Edinburgh

ARMSTRONG'S

14 TEVIOT PLACE · EH1 2QZ · 0131 226 4634
and 64–66 CLERK STREET · EH8 9JB
0131 667 3056

Under the same ownership as Armstrong's in
the Grassmarket, and jealously guarded by
Edinburgh's vintage enthusiasts. A good range
of classic gear at realistic prices.

UNICORN ANTIQUES

65 DUNDAS STREET · EH3 6RS
0131 556 7176 · www.unicornantiques.com

This shabby-chic basement is host to all
manner of trinkets from light fixtures to
mirrors, but it's the costume jewellery in here
that is truly delightful.

ANTIQUES & CURIOS CABARET

137 WEST PORT · EH3 9DP · 0131 229 4100

Another store bursting with edible-looking
costume jewels. It's toatie inside, so do take
care when browsing.

SMOOCH

51 BREAD STREET · EH3 9AH · 0131 228 8787

Eclectic. This store (which is just down a few
doors from Herman Brown) has a strong
personality stamped on it that is unique to
the owner.

COOKIE

29A–31 COCKBURN STREET · EH1 1BP

0131 622 7260

Funky, funky, funky. You'll find it deep in the heart of one of the most vibrant parts of Edinburgh's Old Town. FYI: it's pronounced Co-burn NOT Cock-burn Street.

JOEY D

54 BROUGHTON STREET · EH1 3SA

0131 557 6672 · www.joey-d.co.uk

This designer's client list includes Kimberly Stewart, Paris Hilton and the cast of *Gossip Girl*. He recycles clothing and unusual materials, turning them into bespoke pieces. His handbags alone are worth the trip.

THREADBARE

66A BROUGHTON STREET · EH3 6BJ

www.threadbare-edinburgh.co.uk

Right underneath Joey D's sits the bonniest bijou basement. Be careful on the steps – more than a hundred years of footfall have taken their toll. The owner showcases the best of vintage plus new designers. It's one of my favourites in the city.

BARNARDO'S VINTAGE

116 WEST BOW · GRASSMARKET

29–31 DEANHAUGH STREET · STOCKBRIDGE

Grassmarket Great little vintage charity shop. Always a colourful window display and very creative inside – perhaps explained by the manageress's fine art degree.

Stockbridge Legend has it that the vaults of this store entomb a 1920s flapper dress. It is said an exquisite, grey debutante wanders the New Town, naked, hunting in vain for her beaded black finery.

Both of these stores are well worth a peek. You may strike it lucky and stumble across something truly sensational.

CHARITY SHOP HOP

Gorgie Road to Dalry Road Morningside Road · St Johns Road, Corstorphine · Deanhaugh Street, Stockbridge · George IV Bridge to South Clerk Street · Easter Road

Meet the Stylist...
Zoe Hill

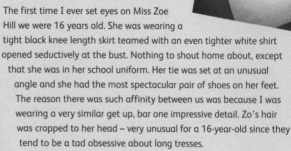

The first time I ever set eyes on Miss Zoe Hill we were 16 years old. She was wearing a tight black knee length skirt teamed with an even tighter white shirt opened seductively at the bust. Nothing to shout home about, except that she was in her school uniform. Her tie was set at an unusual angle and she had the most spectacular pair of shoes on her feet. The reason there was such affinity between us was because I was wearing a very similar get up, bar one impressive detail. Zo's hair was cropped to her head – very unusual for a 16-year-old since they tend to be a tad obsessive about long tresses.

Since those days she has metamorphosed into a fashion designer, make-up artist and stylist. She is the brains behind each city's Look Book, showing how vintage items can be styled for day and night along with modern pieces from your wardrobe to avoid looking like some '70s tribute act.

Zo is my secret weapon and the girl has been attending to my style needs for the past 10 years. If ever I'm in a fashion jam I always think 'what would Zo do?' to avoid wardrobe malfunctions. So I am gifting my secret weapon to you, and trust me when I say you're in safe hands.

Zoe's key to getting vintage right follows a simple set of rules that anyone can follow when she isn't around first hand for a second opinion. These are:

- Find something you love and wear it.
- Don't be afraid to create new looks around the item with other pieces in your wardrobe.
- Accessories are under-used, so don't think about binning your wardrobe, think about how different accessories can change an item of clothing.
- Use your clothes to express yourself. Fashion should be fun and ultimately it should make you feel great.

A Girl's Guide to
Dundee

The City of Discovery is one of our nation's unsung heroes. Known to all that love her as the city built on the three Js – jam, jute and journalism – this unpresuming place puts the Great into Britain. Beautiful reminders of its industrial past dot the landscape as old factories house new identities from clothes stores to quirky accommodation. Its school of fine art is globally respected but seldom shouted about and Dundee United FC have – in my humble opinion – the best shade of football strip in all the SPL.

This tiny city has made a massive impact on how we live today through manufacturing, media and expeditions. Dundee proves size means nothing, it's all about how we use it! Vintage is sporadic here, with some shops open for a couple of days either side of the weekend, but that all adds to Dundee's air of quirkiness. Or as I see it, its artistic flair.

In the '60s Andy Warhol did for art what The Beatles did for music – turned it into popular culture. He bounced from cheap factory to cheap factory in Manhattan, churning out iconic images that we see around us on a daily basis. The factory became just as important as the artist himself. It was the heartbeat of his movement. When you trundle around Dundee you get that same sense, as though the industrial soul of the city has rubbed off on its people, making it quite unlike any other place in the UK. Much like Warhol's Velvet Underground, Dundee has a creative sub culture that thrives off its great art institutions. True, it's still a little rough around the edges but that's what make it interesting. I'm the kind of girl who likes chunks in her peanut butter and pulp in her orange juice – the rougher the better – and that applies to my second-hand. Dundee is vintage with pulp. Delicious.

Look out for: Tomorrow's vintage in the form of the new designers.

Prices: £20 to £3 is average in here.

RARA and The Pretty Vacant Showrooms

29 EXCHANGE STREET · DUNDEE · DD1 3DJ · 0779 44 2 88 75

Now I want to share Dundee's factory with you. Much like Warhol's version, this place is so much more than a space to store canvases. RARA and The Pretty Vacant Showrooms is an epicentre for all things creative. The shop was set up in 2008 by Erin Ward primarily because there were no outlets for her to sell her own things while studying at art school. It became abundantly clear to her that no one was bridging the gap between the creative community in Dundee and its mainstream. So RARA rose.

Each item has a Warhol 'Superstar' quality about it – be it the little Edie dresses dotted around waiting to be danced in or the Lou Reed-esq attire for the lads. It's Andy's most productive decades ('60s to the '80s) that play the leading roles inside the store on Exchange Street. Like the factory's revolving door the store shares this truly eclectic movement by way of the punters it attracts. There isn't an 'average' shopper to be found inside the premises, Rara feels the love from 15-year-old school girls looking for something the high street can't provide to 60-year-old truckers in for a nosy.

On top of Erin's impressive smattering of vintage you'll find new items made from up and coming clothes and jewellery designers that are being nurtured by the city's art schools. To the back of the shop exhibitions are held to help local artists and Erin even runs a magazine called *Jude* from the property. It's a one-stop shop for partying, shopping and culture – all you have to do is turn up.

Look out for: Their website for all the latest info on how to wear current trends with a vintage twist.

Prices: £20 upwards.

Beco Boutique 4 WHITEHALL CRESCENT · DUNDEE · DD1 4AU

01382 220933 · www.becoboutique.com

Reconstruction is the name of the game here, and oh don't they do it well!

Born out of a ground-breaking project to get innovative new businesses into Dundee city centre, Beco is the brain child of Lauris Tosh and her sister Jade Barnett — gals who not only think outside the box but like redesigning them too. 'Project Retail' was spearheaded by Ultimo tycoon Michelle Mone and the Wellgate Centre, where Beco was given free premises for a year.

The Boutique's core beliefs are simple, and sentiments that any true retro lover will understand. They want to steer people away from thinking there must be continual production of new clothing made to meet consumer demands, and instead instill the thought that revamped and recycled clothing should be the way forward. This ethos is stitched into every fibre in-store.

True to the city's form there is something industrial about Beco that gives it a real edgy quality. What's interesting about the items you'll find here is they're chosen in conjunction with current trends, to cater to people who like what they see on the high street but want clothes with a little more soul. Festival time is done fabulously — being so close to T in the Park you should think so too, with customised vintage Levi's jeans cut up into skimpy shorts with embellishments from studs to sequins sewn on.

Look out for: The store front. This is a very small shop – blink and you'll miss it. Also look out for the corsages. Opening hours are a little different than the other vintage shops in the area, it's 12–5 Tuesday to Saturday, so don't be caught out.

Prices: There is a mixture of old and new stock so prices vary. Your starting off point is around £20.

Ms Havisham 55 ALBERT STREET · DUNDEE · DD4 6NY

There once was a lady jilted by her lover at the altar. The wealthy maiden was duped out of her millions by the man she loved. To avoid the pain she simply stopped time; commemorating the exact moment she was told by her beloved he would not be marrying her she set all clocks to twenty minutes to nine. From that day forward she stayed indoors, dressed in her wedding gown with one shoe slipped on a single foot. Her tortured soul would never find true happiness – even on her death bed – but on the bright side, at least she was wearing a knock-out dress! The lady of Dundee's Ms Havisham is far from Dickens' fateful heroine, however, their only similarity is their insistence on formal wear.

Up a sweeping hill on Albert Street is where you'll find our final treat. A handful of charity shops lead the way – but if you hit a sex shop you've gone astray. Elke, owner of Ms Havisham, has a flair for all things wonderful. This gal is from the old school where girls dressed like ladies and took pride in their appearance, so when you touch base with this place that is what to expect. A fabric bazaar holding old and new items, it has clothing sliding from every spare space, showing Dundee can give Hollywood a run for its money when it comes to the glamour stakes.

Everything you will find in-store has been loved by Elke, a mantra that the shop is run on, after all if she doesn't love it then why would she ask you to!

Ms Havisham is the essence of femininity. If you embrace that along with anything that sparkles you'll most certainly find a kindred spirit in our Elke for it radiates from her and the shop. Her personal decades of decadence are the 1920s and '30s but you'll find a larger range of items spanning the '60s to present day. A woman's touch is what's in practice here and it makes you proud of our wily female ways.

The Dundee
look book

Day

Night

The List
Dundee

Dundee isn't one of our largest cities for vintage shopping, but what it lacks in bespoke vintage stores it makes up for in authentic charity shop shopping. Find your way to the largest roads in Dundee and stumble across the pick of our country's biggest charity chains. Never underestimate how good a peek around a charity shop can be when it comes to trying to uncover a vintage gem. But since I like to make your life easy, here is a list of the shops you should definitely get to know when you are in Dundee...

AGE CONCERN LTD
10 CONSTITUTION ROAD · DD1 1LL

BRITISH HEART FOUNDATION
14 REFORM STREET · DD1 1RG

BARNARDO'S
55 REFORM STREET · DD1 1SP
14 DUDHOPE STREET · DD1 1JU
1 DUDHOPE TERRACE · DD3 6HG

BRITISH RED CROSS SOCIETY
314 PERTH ROAD · DD2 1AU

CANCER RESEARCH UK
2A HIGHGATE CENTRE
102 HIGH STREET · DD2 3BL

CAPABILITY SCOTLAND
182 BROOK STREET · DD5 2AH

DUNDEE AGE CONCERN
CAIRD AVENUE · DD3 8AW

OXFAM
71 HIGH STREET · DD2 3AT
202 BROOK STREET · DD5 2AH

PDSA
125 HIGH STREET · DD2 3BX

SHELTER
268 PERTH ROAD · DD2 1AE

THE RETIRED GREYHOUND TRUST
66 ALBERT STREET · DD4 6QH

CHARITY SHOP HOP
Albert Street · High Street · Perth Street

George Lamb

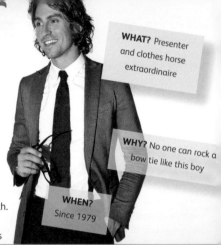

Clothes are all about expressing yourself. They tell the world who you are before you've even opened your mouth. Sometimes people get it, other times you're left to deal with gawping gazes as you saunter on by. It's like your signature, your fingerprints, your eye colour. Completely unique to you. Some people embrace their individuality while others feel far more comfortable being beige.

George Lamb is far from beige. If you're unsure of his fashion credentials the best way to sum him up is as the male equivalent of Carrie Bradshaw. Pure eccentricity and manicured tailoring. With one minor difference, instead of Patricia Field helping pick out looks it's his boy Sauvage.

But this quirky dress sense that has landed him in many a best-dressed list is as much down to inheritance as it is free will and great styling. You see, there's one man who stands out in George's family tree, a shining example in the world of dapper dresser-dom. That man was George Martin fae Dundee. Or Grandpa to George.

Every summer when George was a boy he'd head to Dundee for the holidays. Waiting at the train station for him with a disappointed look on his face stood Grandpa Martin, as George bounded towards him with floppy locks blowing freely in the Baltic breeze. First thing was always a visit to the barbers. No grandson of his was going to be running around town with hair like that! You have to look presentable after all.

The stonemason was famous for never leaving the house in anything less than perfection. Even if that meant nipping down to the shop for a pint of milk. Crisp white shirts and ties were placed underneath immaculate suits. Trilbies and brogues were the hard hat and steel toe cap of choice for Mr Martin when he headed to work. From the way things have turned out it looks like little floppy-haired George picked up more than just his grandfather's name.

A Girl's Guide to
Aberdeen

I'm convinced the creators of *Dallas* did a spell in Aberdeen, coining the programme that defined a decade from the oil-rich soils of the Silver City. Sue Ellen has to be based on an Aberdonian glamazon married to some nasty womanising billionaire that treats her contemptibly. The city still maintains the excess of the '80s, its money-hungry ethos burning as brightly as the flames on the rigs. Here they work hard and play harder, and their vintage is an homage to the style and razor-sharp tailoring of this exorbitant epoch.

Dubbed the decade taste disposed of, the 1980s can only be described as the Marmite of fashion. Loved or loathed, this chapter divides more of the sisterhood than any other. The fashion forward lap it up while the rest look on bewildered. If Laver's timeline stands you define this decade as ridiculous or amusing. If not, chances are you live in Aberdeen or you'll love it up here.

Personally I think the '80s gets a raw deal, sure there were a couple of unforgivable manoeuvres on the fashion checker board but I think it's time to banish the memories of poodle perms and scrunchies that matched your ra-ra skirt and rejoice in the resurrection of Jean

Muir, the birth of Vivienne Westwood and Karl Lagerfeld taking the helm of Chanel. Of course Aberdeen has more to offer its vintage explorer than threads from this specific time, but they do it so well I'd be a fool not to shout about it.

The Blossoming Scene

Aberdeen isn't bursting at the seams with vintage. It is a growing scene, one that already has a very strong identity. While plotting your shopping path for the day you will find yourself veering to places organically. There's a handful of top-notch vintage stores in the city centre, the rest of your vintage comes courtesy of charity shops.

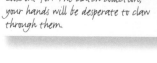

Look out for: The clutch collection, your hands will be desperate to claw through them.

Prices: From £5 handbags to dresses from £25 upwards. Special pieces range around the £80 mark. You can even hire clothes here.

The Closet JOPPS LANE · ABERDEEN · AB25 1BX · 01224 625 450

www.closet-vintage.co.uk

Heading to The Closet can feel remarkably similar to the sensation that slides through your stomach the minute you arrange to meet an illicit lover. Undetectable to the naked eye, the store is ambiguously tucked away at the bottom of Jopps Lane. You find yourself glancing over your shoulder as you edge closer to The Closet, determined to keep your passion under wraps a few moments longer. Every female that visits instantly reverts to her dark side. Desperate to keep it all to herself, the secret is only shared with those she truly trusts.

The sensual surroundings make for a pleasurable peruse. Show stopping '8os pieces are pinned to the walls, sprinkled in old suitcases and showcased on mannequins. Brigitte Bardot smoulders from a framed photo above the clothes racks, granting good style fortune to all that shop below her. The feeling of feminine fierceness that courses through your body as you glide your hands over the vibrant '8os

dresses is all consuming. The bold shapes and structures, mixed with magnificent fabrics, instantly unleash your inner Pam Ewing.

Handwritten notes are pinned to each garment like tiny forget-me-nots, introducing you to each outfit. You can't help but fall head-over-heels with the sequin collection lovingly hand-picked by Terrie, the glamorous American manageress. What she doesn't know about vintage isn't worth thinking about. The LA gal has been doing this longer than she cares to remember, even though she looks dangerously like a teen. Her chilled-out bohemian attitude radiates through the place like the Californian sun on silver sands. The Closet will leave you glowing with guilty pleasure and scribbling a date in your diary for the next rendezvous.

RetroSpect

Look out for: The badge collection at the cash desk

Prices: On average £30.

Alitalia

BRACES
£6 each
or
2 for £1...

Retrospect

9 ST ANDREW STREET · ABERDEEN · AB25 1BQ · 01224 631 278
www.retrovintageclothing.co.uk

A kaleidoscope of colour rushes to mind when I think of Retrospect. Walking into this vintage rainbow is a bit like the moment Dorothy discovers Oz. Stumbling out from her black and white shackles for the first time, encounting the glory of Technicolor. Much like Dorothy, Retrospect has it's very own Tin Man gallantly guiding your gallivanting. Steven took over the shop at the tail end of 2008. His vintage pedigree is illustrious. He'll be the first to tell you his real passion is vintage glass in all guises, the stuff really gets his heart a-flutter, but it's the clothes inside his store that gets mine.

Unconventionally, gals have to walk through the guys' section at the front of the shop to get to the goodies. This is a treat in my opinion since I'm a big fan of men's shirts, they look fantastic over the most feminine of outfits. Checked shirts reign supreme and you'll find representations from all nations on the silver racks. Eastern European brushes against Americana deliciously.

Once you tear yourself from the men's threads it's off to the back of the shop for some more Eastern promise. Here German and Czech garments feed Aberdeen's hunger for all things '80s. The selection of prom dresses you can choose from will make your day, all froufrou and velvety-soft, a microcosm of the decade. It's the fact Steve looks further afield for his vintage that makes this place remarkable. So save yourself the air fare and jet lag and get up to Aberdeen for a spot of shopping Retrospectivestylie.

CHILDREN 1ST

Look out for: The staff, they couldn't be nicer.

Prices: Outfits and dresses for under a tenner.

Children 1st
191 GEORGE STREET · ABERDEEN · AB25 1HX · 01224 622 814
www.children1st.org.uk

Conjure Michelle Pfeiffer circa *Scarface* playing cocaine ice queen Elvira as she struts seductively in that powder-white power suit, all shoulder padded splendour and cinched waist. Her skirt split sensationally thighwards in white peep-toed stilettos and those outrageously chic sunglasses. Or muse over Melanie Griffith's ditzy but determined Tess McGill, as she turns her boss's closet upside down trying on black velvet Dior with a sprinkling of sequins in *Working Girl*. Only then are you ready to sample the stash at my next store. It's almost like these ladies have dropped the clothes off there themselves.

 Now I really didn't think a charity shop would feature in any of my top three city finds, but there was no chance I could keep this to myself. Charity shops are king in Aberdeen. I think it's down to the bursting wardrobes of rich women and the healthy influx of students annually. Whatever it is, Children 1st certainly benefits from the generosity of donors and the loyalty of certain stylish women to its cause.

The sheer beauty of this charity shop is just that. It is still a charity shop. Nothing is colour-coordinated or showcased in fancy displays. You come here for a good old root around. Any time I am there I beg the staff not to conform to current trends of turning classic charity shops into soulless stores desperate to squeeze every last penny out of their donated goods by escalating their prices. They duly promise. On my last visit I found a fresh shipment of '80s Laura Ashley and Jaeger. Fabulous. The greatest thing about this place is much like Forrest Gump's famous catchphrase: a charity shop is indeed like a box of chocolates. You never know what you're gonna get.

Night

Tartan & Leopard Print

Two of my favourite prints are animal and tartan. Individually they make a fierce statement and are frequently featured on the fashion faithful. Some might even say the patterns are the uniform of the hip and trendy – and who am I to disagree with that? There's only one thing that can trump them and that's when you team the two together. This look isn't for the fashion faint hearted – it's for the female who is confident in her choices and isn't afraid to clash. It's for the girl in touch with her inner rock chick.

My national dress has always played a massive part in my life – from being forced into itchy tartan dresses as a child to finding my first pair of Pringle golf trousers in a charity shop. Our relationship has had some bumps in the road, but we're stronger because of the struggles. The material was originally worn by clansmen to identify which family they belonged to when in battle. Our Irish cousins will never fail to tell you that we pinched tartan from them. Now fashion brands from House of Holland to Vivienne Westwood have adopted it, transforming it into iconic clobber.

The love affair with leopard print could be said to be embedded in our psyche from our hunter-gatherer days. Originally regarded as a status symbol – furs were draped over African men with royal blood – now we have the option to replicate the most intricate of animal print for people not so fortunate. The look screams old Hollywood glamour, never failing to make you feel like a screen siren every time you slide it on.

Loving or loathing the prints is a clear indication on where you stand in the fashion barometer. Tipping the love scales is a deep indication that you are a fashion junkie – and proud to be so.

ROSEHIP AND TUTU

197 ROSEMOUNT PLACE · AB25 2XP

01224 622 522 · www.rosehip-tutu.co.uk

Waste not want not is the ethos at this store. Vintage is lovingly recreated into new outfits instore. They are also partial to a wee shindig here, dress-swapping parties are held here every week. Very eco-friendly, prices can vary but you'll find them middle of the road.

CANDLE CLOSE GALLERY

1ST FLOOR · 123 GALLOWGATE · AB25 1BU

01224 624 940 · www.candleclosegallery.co.uk

Was torn in my decision not to put this in my top three. The reason it didn't make it is because you won't find vintage clothes per se. Here you can find recycled clothes remastered into new items along-side show-stopping pieces of antique furniture. The inside of this building is truly breathtaking.

CHARITY SHOP HOP

George Street · King Street

A Girl's Guide to
Glasgow

There's no place like home. I was born and bred in Glasgow's Merchant City and spent every weekend immersed in the old Fruitmarket or rooting around The Barras. My favourite childhood memories are eating mussels with my father in one of the seafood cafes, watching the traders go about their business, or being transfixed by the glass cabinets of my mother's favourite jewellery stalls. I never left disappointed, or empty-handed.

From the hip boutiques of the West End to the gritty streets of Calton, Glasgow harbours some of the best places for vintage in the UK. There's no excuse, you have to come and spend at least a weekend here and explore it for yourself.

The Fairy Godmother of Vintage
The trio I'm about to entrust to you represent the real, raw Glasgow – salt of the earth with bags of style. The woman who made it all a reality is Margaret Russell, the founder of the now world famous Barras. I'm not sure the other vintage stores in Glasgow would be around today had she not mapped the way. Margaret embodied the entrepreneurial spirit. She set up

The Barras street market at the turn of the 20th century and expanded her empire with the Barrowlands Ballroom shortly thereafter. I have a lot of family history stored around the stalls – my great aunties once sold clothes at this very market.

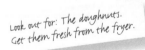

Look out for: The doughnuts.
Get them fresh from the fryer.

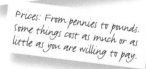

Prices: From pennies to pounds.
Some things cost as much or as
little as you are willing to pay.

The Barras GALLOWGATE · GLASGOW · G1 5AX · 0141 552 4601

www.glasgowbarrowland.com

Zig-zagging from stall to stall you get a real feel for how the place would have looked when Maggie ruled the roost. Old warehouses and cobbled streets are the backdrop for market stalls. It's a diamond in the rough, and I hope it never changes. You can find everything here, including the kitchen sink. It's an Aladdin's Cave of pet shops and plant nurseries, butchers and furniture makers, toy shops and jewellery displays, paintings and fireplaces, carpets and books – but it's the clothes that get me in a kerfuffle. I've seen myself part with my last 20 quid all because I'd fallen in love with something that just had to come home with me. On one occasion, a 1950s chiffon evening gown with feather sleeves captured my heart, and made my bosoms defy gravity.

Some might say the market is not what it once was, but I think they're buying into an urban myth. The interior may have seen better days, but its shabbiness is part of its charm. While the rest of the city went through urban regeneration, The Barras stayed true to itself. All Glasgow life is here.

My tips for successful shopping are simple. Come early and drink in the atmosphere. Grab a roll and square sausage from one of the cafes, then lose yourself in the old warehouses and stalls.

Feel free to haggle. Even if you think you're going to hate it, give it a whirl. Talk to the traders. Some of them have been there all their lives and their stories can be riveting. Stay until the traders begin packing up in the late afternoon, when you're more likely to snap up a steal of a deal. Play Barras Bingo – if I spot something in the morning only to return to find it's gone, then it wasn't meant to be. If your beloved is still there, the Barras' gods clearly want you to be united.

Prices: Dresses range from £18 to £80. There's a budget for everyone.

Look out for: The biker jackets.

48

Mr Ben 101 KING STREET · GLASGOW · G1 5RB · 0141 553 1936

www.mrbenretroclothing.com

In a forgotten pocket of the Merchant City lies the hippest arcade in town, where Glasgow's creative types descend like moths to a flame. With over 10 years in the business, there's nothing owner Mary Anne King doesn't know about fashion. Cutting her teeth at The Barras, she went on to transform Mr Ben into *the* place for vintage. A bit like drinking the best espresso, you get an instant buzz the second your feet hit the shop floor.

Every item of stock has been personally approved by Mary Anne – no mean feat inside a cavernous, converted railway arch. Her shoe collection is the most impressive I've ever come across in my vintage travels, with the cowboy boots the stars of the show. The dresses also fire me up. I could bathe in the fabrics forever, splashing around in the 1950s or diving headlong into the '80s.

After a satisfying afternoon of trying and buying, grab yourself a well-deserved drink in Mono a few doors down and soak up the atmosphere in this eclectic neck of the woods.

Look out for: The haberdashery.

Prices: The secondhand furs are the most expensive stock – between £40 and £60.

Starry Starry Night 19 DOWANSIDE LANE · GLASGOW · G12 9BZ
0141 337 1837

A trip on The Clockwork Orange, Glasgow's Underground, takes you to our next port of call. Alight at Hillhead in the leafy West End, and head for Dowanside Lane, right across the road from the subway exit. Cobbles guide you to the entrance of a quaint cabin, painted evergreen. Open the wooden door and be catapulted to the vintage version of Narnia. The scent of old clothes and dark wood is so delicious I wish someone would bottle it. Low lights and an even lower ceiling create an intimate atmosphere, verging on the opulent. Bundles of bib and tucker are so tightly packed, it's a wonder there's room for the staff, let alone customers. Moving sideways should aid your navigation. Like a giant game of Jenga, you may fret that removing even the most insignificant rag runs the risk of bringing down the house, leaving you clutching the incriminating evidence. Don't be put off. I can assure you the place is made of sturdier stuff, so get stuck in.

You will unearth a diverse mix of clothing and accessories from the '20s to the '90s – but it's Anna's coats which are the most alluring. On my last visit I picked up two capes – I just couldn't choose between them. One is a chocolate brown and cream Donegal tweed that came to Glasgow via Dublin in the 1960s. The second is a 1940s lammas wool creation from a department store in Edinburgh called Darlings, sadly no longer with us. Both set me back £20. That's what I call a bargain.

The Glasgow
look book

WEST END

WE LOVE TO BOOGIE
100 BYRES RD · G12 8TB · 0141 339 2577
85 ST GEORGE'S ROAD · G3 6JA
0141 564 1396
www.welovetoboogievintage.com

My most fashionable friends practically live
in these stores. You can have your vintage
from the 1890s to the 1990s in here. Our very
own stylist Ms Zoe Hill has a serious weakness
for this place and you only have to visit to
see why.

HANDBAGS AND GLADRAGS
158 DUMBARTON ROAD · PARTICK · G1 2JZ
(next to Kelvinhall Underground)

Splendour hangs from every wall. A great
selection of garments from the early 1990s.

WATERMELON
603 GREAT WESTERN ROAD · G12 8HX
0141 334 3900
www.myspace.com/watermelon_clothing

Vintage of the laid-back variety. Very warm
and friendly service and the pieces are
awesome. Another must-see store.

RETRO
8 OTAGO STREET · KELVINBRIDGE · G12 8JH
0141 576 0165
www.retro-clothes.com

Dazzling selection from the '50s to the '70s,
covering summer dresses to winter coats,
accessories and shoes. It's a favourite of
mine and the locals.

CIRCA VINTAGE
37 RUTHVEN LANE · OFF BYRES ROAD
G12 9BG · 0141 334 6660
www.circavintage.co.uk

Very nearly made it into my top three. Sheila
Murdoch is another of Glasgow's great
vintage sellers who started off down The
Barras. I adore her cocktail dresses and boots.

THE GLORY HOLE
41 RUTHVEN LANE · G12 9BG
0141 357 5662

Part of the vintage village tucked behind
Byres Road, this little store has personality-
a-plenty and the potential for a good poke
around.

SOUTH SIDE

RAW VINTAGE
3 ABBOT STREET · G41 3XE · 0141 649 2752
www.recycleandwear.co.uk

A 20-minute bus trip from the city centre
seems a small price to pay for a slice of
Shawlands' style.

CITY CENTRE

SARATOGA TRUNK
61 HYDEPARK STREET · G3 8BW
0141 221 4433
www.saratogatrunk.co.uk

Oodles of clothes to buy and hire. A one-stop
shop for local burlesque troupe Club Noir.

BRIGITTE
41 KING STREET · G1 5RA · 0141 552 9564

High-end designer vintage that will leave you
weak at the knees. The clothes are simply
scrumptious, and that is reflected in the
prices.

BARNARDO'S BOUTIQUE
54 WILSON STREET · G1 1HD
0141 552 9581
www.barnardos.org.uk

Guilt-free charity shopping in a great
location. Stock tends to change day to day.

CHARITY SHOP HOP
High Street onto Saltmarket · Duke
Street · Byres Road · Great Western
Road · Partick Cross

Loulabelle
Superstar

WHO? Mhari Louise 'Lou' Hickey, 26

WHAT? Singer/Song-writer supremo

WHERE? Glasgow

WHEN? Since 1983

WHY? Crowned Scotland's most eligible female, her cute clothing even nabbed her band 'Most Stylish Band' during the 2009 Style Awards

Lou Hickey's smoky vocals evoke the atmosphere of a jazz bar, somewhere in the middle of Paris, circa 1952. She oozes old school, from the pin-up dresses to the purring delivery. Her look and sound may be a nod to the past, but Lou manages to pull it off with a freshness that keeps it cutting edge. If Billie Holiday, Edith Piaf, Dusty Springfield and Marilyn Monroe were reduced to their essence, there would be Lou. Signed to Island the year the record company turned 50, she writes with the wisdom of a woman twice her age. If you are an alumni of the burlesque scene, you will already be familiar with her sashaying stage persona, Loulabelle.

Lou fully embraced vintage when she first starting performing at Club Noir in Glasgow in 2004. In that time she has racked up innumerable costume changes and song choices, but one thing has remained a constant, and you might notice it the next time you see her. A 1930s diamanté bracelet is her most treasured vintage possession, owned by her grandmother before her. 'I always had my eye on the piece, but my mother kept it under lock and key. She finally passed it on to me two years ago, even though I'd been secretly wearing it long before that. It's a small connection to a woman who has shaped so much of my life, without us ever meeting.' You get the impression that the apple has not fallen too far from the tree.

A Girl's Guide to *Belfast*

The Emerald Isle is caboose to some of my most cherished commodities in the country. It is here the other half was born and raised, it is where you'll find my best friend Steph residing, and it is the place my beautiful nephews rest their weary little heads after a hard day's play. I have made magnificent memories here over the years, not to mention that it's provided me with valued vintage vestments bestowed by my Belfast boy's grandmother, Lily. Steeped in history – some good, some bad, some ugly – the city has a vibrance and resilience like no other in the UK. And even though it pains me to say this, as it feels like I'm giving up my secret vintage stash, Belfast is the best place for untapped vintage shopping across the country. So get a pint of the black stuff down you, try a packet of Tayto cheese and onion crisps, say hello to two of Belfast's biggest icons, Samson and Goliath (the Harland and Wolff cranes that watched *The Titanic* being built beneath them) and head off for the best craic you'll ever encounter while out for an afternoon's shopping.

Look out for: The shirt collection
— not as extensive as the denim
and leather sections but well
worth a shout.

Prices: £30 can get you a feast. Jeans
for a tenner and bins filled to the
rims to be raided for a fiver. Leather
jackets from £30.

Mike Hunt HI PARK CENTRE · HIGH ST · BELFAST · BT1 2JZ · 028 9031 4155

Hot patootie, bless my soul I really love that rock and roll!

Tucked away from the trendier places to part with a pound you'll find yourself thinking that somehow you've tripped into a time warp. That vulnerability Brad and Janet must-have felt as they knocked on Dr Frank-N-Furter's front door that fateful evening floods your brain and courses through your veins as the 'In Shop' sign to the Hi-Park Centre becomes visible. Looking around to make sure no mistakes have been made before disappearing into the '80s brickwork, a twinge of doubt plagues you. People have spoken about the great Mike Hunt – but now you're not sure if you've been sent on a wild goose chase.

Passing by store after store until you can't take no more, Mike shows himself and you are utterly in awe. Much like Meatloaf's character Eddie in *Rocky Horror*, Mike Hunt is totally the star of this show. Unashamedly masculine, Mike Hunt looks like Eddie's – and Meatloaf's – kinda place with biker jackets in all shade of leather. So much denim you'd swear a cowboy convention had just convened and camouflage failing to fade into the background peppers the rest of the surroundings. Original Levi's 501 signs swing above the impressive jean range coordinated by size. For all those wannabe rock gods Mike Hunt raises his goblet of rock in the form of a glittering array of vintage band Ts. From AC/DC to Nirvana and everything else in between, your hands will suffer severe cramp by the time you've thumbed through the lot.

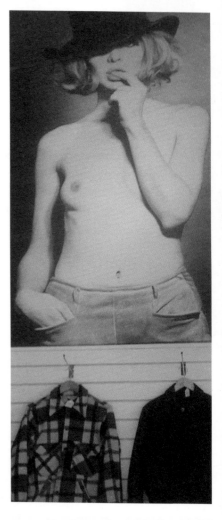

Look out for: The topless pictures on the wall – arty to a T.

Prices: Your pound won't go as far here as some other places but whatever you come away with will be with you for life. £40 is around average.

Bang Boutique 13 CHURCH LANE · BELFAST · BT1 4QN
www.bangboutique.co.uk

Belfast's own take on Barbarella can be found at Bang. A mixture between comic books come to life and Jane Fonda's sexy spaceship makes you feel like you've stumbled by some sci-fi convention for cool kids. The styling is out of this world and it's the best place to come face to face with Belfast's signature *savoir-faire*. Their style is a massive melting pot of looks, pulling influences from glamour, rock, mod and modern day attire. This funky fusion is completely unique to the natives but easily transferable so you don't look out of place wearing their gear wherever you may be.

Bang is best described as an art installation that you become part of as you walk around. There are many relics of interest worthy of pulling your attention away from the clothes. The cash desk is an original shop fixture from the '60s that had to be delivered in two pieces, and upstairs old magazines sit on top of an ancient telly box. I don't usually fall for shop fixtures when there's vintage shopping to be had but the items inside Bang are truly worth the time it takes for a good gawk.

Tight band Ts teamed with even tighter pencil skirts should keep the ladies occupied while the men have a dapper selection of shirts from mod to checked. The stock has been damage controlled to the boss's liking which means there is a really high calibre of clothing to look through. It also doesn't sit on the rails for very long, as the team understand the importance of rotating stock. This approach works well at keeping the shop as fresh and hip as its interior. Ten minutes in here and you'll come out feeling like the coolest kid at school.

Rusty Zip

retro and vintage clothing   tel 9024 9700

Look out for: All the postcards and pictures stuck up in the dressing rooms.

Prices: start off around £30 upwards. Really special pieces you can expect to pay a little more for.

62

Rusty Zip
28 BOTANIC AVENUE · BELFAST · BT7 1JQ · 028 9024 9700
www.therustyzip.com

Heading out of the city to the student quarters and home of the Botanic Gardens, a classic little vintage joint hits the spot rightly after a hard day's shop. Belfast's bohemian heartbeat runs through Botanic Avenue but unfortunately it doesn't generate the same exposure as some places round town due to the fact that it isn't a polar opposite or stereotype. A 10-minute walk from City Hall up Dublin Street sees you right at the doorstep of the leafier side of town, a place so pleasurable you could pound the pavements for prolonged periods without ever feeling the pain in your feet.

Prince's 'Purple Rain' would be my theme tune of choice for Rusty Zip, its violaceous haze conjuring Jimi Hendrix it's so deliciously psychedelic. Like leaving the best first date you've ever been on, Rusty Zip gives you butterflies and smiles, filling you with a nervous energy that makes you want to leap out of your clothes and into someone else's. That '60s air of free love still hangs off the garments, giving the shop the sweetest taboo.

Phenomenal paraphernalia is propped everywhere but it's the clobber that is truly paramount. Belfast has this wicked way of making you fall in love with it – that's why I ended up with a man and a best mate from there! – and it is no different with these clothes. Fun frocks oozing with personality will have you painstakingly peering over them as you try and decide which ones you want. Then come the coats… full-length suedes with fluffy trims look like they have just been looted from Ms Patti Boyd's Beatles wardrobe. Old photos and fliers are blu-tacked to the walls in the changing room, adding to that bohemian spirit in the street. Clothes are stacked well above head height, creating grandeur in the narrow store. For anyone who missed out on living in the '60s and '70s I imagine this is what it would feel like – and for that insight alone RZ is a champion of vintage.

Night

Behind every great woman..

WHO? Lily Miskimmin

WHEN? Since 1932

WHAT? Head of the Miskimmin household

WHERE? Belfast

WHY? Because she bought vintage when it was brand new

there's a greater wardrobe

There is a very exclusive spot on the fringes of Belfast city centre to which only a select few are privy.

Dubbed 'Parkmount Stores' to those who know and love it, to the untrained eye the house appears to be an unlikely place for fashion. That is, until you come face to face with Don Lilyleon – The Godfather of vintage.

Head of the Miskimmin household, she is the beloved grandmother of my boyfriend Neal – and the greatest untapped resource of vintage clothing I have ever uncovered.

I have pilfered innumerable ensembles from this lady's wardrobe and each one means the world to me. Any time I am complimented wearing her emerald-green floor-length frock I'm filled with warm thoughts of the woman who gave it to me. I feel comforted each Christmas tucked inside her chocolate-coloured beaver coat away from the harsh winter winds. But best of all I burst with joy each time I relay the stories of how I got my hands on such rare finds.

Your ticket to the best of UK vintage doesn't have to be in far-flung places, it can be right underneath your nose. All you have to do is ask the fabulous older women in your life to open up their wardrobes, and all those untold vintage treasures will be yours.

A Girl's Guide to

Newcastle

The Angel of the North points the way to the home of the country's most exquisite vintage experience. Newcastle is a compact city, and just as well, since the stores I'm about to share deserve hours of your undivided attention lavished upon them. It's a spot for serious vintage lovers, the ones who delight in the craftsmanship of clothes from another world. Cast clock-watching aside. Don't rush, you'll be doing yourself and the city a disservice otherwise. Relax and enjoy every garment like it was your last vintage supper.

Red Windmill

A secret society subsists within the streets of the Toon. Flourishing in the back alleys of the Cloth Market, it can be found down cobbled roads, away from the hustle and bustle of the high street. Turning off Grey Street feels like momentarily meandering into the wrong part of Montmartre in Paris. Instead of the Moulin Rouge staring back at you, an unlikely watering hole, The Beehive, becomes the focal point guiding you to Newcastle's veiled vintage. It is here, shrouded in mystery, where you will find the country's inaugural vintage store.

Look out for: The beautiful etched mirror on the staircase, it turns any ugly sister into Cinderella.

Prices: The rarity and superb condition of Stephen's eveningwear is reflected in his pricing, starting from £40 up to £200. These are outfits you're never going to part with.

Attica

You know when you are in the presence of a star. A spellbinding aura surrounds it, drawing you closer. It's intangible, a quality attained from a higher power. Attica has this enigmatic ambience in abundance. She is the prima ballerina of vintage. From the moment the door closes behind you the dance begins.

Like the Viennese Waltz, feather-light fabrics gently guide you around the room as if you're in the arms of Rudolf Nureyev. Immaculate dresses are draped in order of decade, momentarily you feel like his iconic dance partner Dame Margot Fonteyn. Clouds of chiffon from the '50s and '60s fill the room, with each era showcased to the highest calibre. That intimate feeling you get on the dance floor as your partner sweeps you round is captured as you caress the clothes.

Enhancing Old George Yard since 1992, Attica's owner Stephen Pierce is vintage's answer to dance ace Hermes Pan, the man who taught Fred Astaire and Ginger Rogers how to move. Much like Pan's ability to make Fred and Ginger's feet appear to never touch the ground, Pierce's eye for vintage pieces is unrivalled and can leave you with that floating on air feeling. Screen goddesses await your presence upstairs, their pictures are plastered up in two fairy-lit fitting rooms. Slipping into one of Stephen's hand-picked gowns makes you fit right in with the Hollywood menagerie as Elizabeth Taylor and Rita Hayworth look on approvingly. It's easy to kiss goodbye to an afternoon once inside. The place is like a glamorous Tardis, time evaporates amidst a cloud of Attica perfection.

MENSWEAR
& ACCESSORIES
UPSTAIRS

Best Vintage

Look out for: The table near the staircase cluttered with shoes.

Prices: I'd average it out at about £20
per item.

Best Vintage
14 HIGH BRIDGE · NEWCASTLE UPON TYNE · TYNE AND WEAR
NE1 1EN · 0191 261 8500 · www.bestvintageuk.com

Funky music crashes into your eardrums, vibrating down your spine, making you want to throw down some of your nastiest dance moves as you mince your way around the marvels at Best Vintage. A mere metre from The Beehive lies Soloman's flagship store. With a chain of Bests under his belt, it's his first-born that bowls me over. The whole place rocks, literally as the sound system moves the room. Classic party pieces pinch the spotlight from the convention of daywear. You get the impression a cat fight could break out at any minute as both vie for your attention. They are so consumed by one another they don't realise their biggest competition comes in the form of the '60s coats. All sheepskin and classically British, they just don't make 'em like that anymore.

Women at the front, men in the back is how this store rolls. Shoes and bags bridge the gap between genders. Relaxed funky shopping is what to expect from Best. That is, until you find yourself upstairs. Odd goings on have been reported in the floor above Best's head. The room that houses stock and two disused fitting rooms has more of a paranormal vibe than the chilled out notes below. A man in uniform is said to wander around guarding the property. So if you find yourself up there trying on some party threads, make sure you pull the curtains!

Retro
CLOTHING

Look out for: The sweatshirts, they are a sweet treat.

Prices: £15 is the base entry vintage.

Retro Clothing

29 HIGH BRIDGE · NEWCASTLE UPON TYNE · TYNE AND WEAR · NE1 1EN · 0191 232 5514

Images of grandeur should be generated when painting a mental picture of Retro. Victorian glory greets you in the small foyer where enamel emerald tiles decorate the walls and mosaic flooring goes underfoot. Inside, the most extraordinary stained glass window takes pride of place above the cash desk. The curvature and creativity it captures defines femininity, giving off a great sensation for shopping. It is fitting that latter-day lovelies should be sold beneath its ceilings. The synergy of selling old clothes in this old building is palpable.

A mixture of reworked vintage, new creations and authentic second-hand can be found to fondle, and although vast in ceiling height there's not much floor space to go round with every piece of available room earmarked for items. The store is crammed with dresses, boots, bags, tops and denims, some pieces doubled up to take advantage of that ceiling height.

Daytime clobber is what really catches the eye in Retro. Plus it's a great little place to find something unique with the selection of reworked vintage. Retro's owners Cath and Dave have an individuality that seeps through every facet of their business, from their location to their stock. Quirkiness is queen here.

The Newcastle
look book

Night

Newcastle

BETWEEN THE BUTTONS
15–17 VINE LANE · NE1 7PW
www.betweenthebuttons.com

This is the coolest vintage store in Newcastle.
Set above Newcastle's legendary Steel
Wheels music emporium, the clothing is
tainted with that rock'n'roll edge. Guy's stock
is superb with great going-out shirts and
tracky tops a-plenty.

FLIP
104 WESTGATE ROAD · NE1 4AF
0191 233 1755
www.flip-clothing.co.uk

One of the first stores bringing American
vintage into the UK, Flip has been trading
since the '70s. You can fill your boots on
American brands from Hawaiian shirts to
baseball jackets. There used to be a store in
Glasgow but now it is sadly missed.

CHARITY SHOP HOP

You will find a scattering of charity
shops around the city centre, but head
to Nun Street and Clayton Street for a
more concentrated selection.

WHO? Wayne Hemingway

WHERE? International, baby

WHAT? Designer and cofounder of Red Or Dead

WHEN? Since 1961

WHY? because my life-lo shoe obsession began af purchasing my very first of high heels designed l this man

Wayne

Wonder

Be upstanding for our First Family of Fashion. The Hemingways are national treasures. The man at the helm of the Hemingway household is Wayne. Together with his wife Geradine this dynamic duo have become a creative force to be reckoned with. From selling his nan's handmade '50s frocks down Camden Market in the '80s to forging forward with their own label, Red Or Dead, the pair have accumulated along the way a collection of vintage so tasty it will have your mouth watering.

It was at a jumble sale at the tender age of 18 when Wayne was united with one of his most beloved vintage belongings. The knitted blue ship emblazoned on a sea of cream drew him in like a drunken sailor to gin. Parting with 20 pence, the iconic Blue Peter jumper came home with him.

Nearly four decades on he's still in love with it. But it's more than the jumper's kitsch factor that keeps him keen. It evokes a memory and holds a legacy. He freely admits his vintage obsession would leave the average woman aghast, it's so vast, with wardrobes in each of his homes across the kingdom crammed full of clothes from days gone by.

Vintage is everywhere for Wayne. The wonders of secondhand were passed down from his nan to his mum., from his mum to him. Now he passes the vintage flag on for his daughters to fly. The girls wear dresses made by their great-nan's fair hand. Keeping it in the family has never been more chic.

A Girl's Guide to
Leeds

Leeds has been keeping a secret from the rest of us and I'm about to expose it. West Yorkshire's finest isn't their puddings, it's their threads. The home of Marks and Spencer and The Dalek Building has the most impressive range collectively of top quality vintage in the UK. You'll need to buy yourself a bus ticket, for I'm taking you to the four corners of the city, leaving no vintage stone unturned.

The Real Reason

Stop to ask the average person on the streets of Leeds why they are dubbed Loiners and you'll get differing answers. Some think its roots derive from the eighth century name for the district, Loidis. Others believe it's down to the yards and closes around Briggate known as Low Ins or Loins. Then there's my personal favourite, the term was given to the gossips who hung around said yards and closes. I, however, have another definition for the Loiner. They stand alone in the style stakes, embracing individuality and celebrating vintage in its highest form. For that reason I feel it is only fair to prepare you for its pricing. It can be expensive, but once witnessed you'll understand why.

Look out for: The light pink leopard print suitcase housing display stock.

Prices: £40 is the average jumping off point. These are one-offs, the more unique the higher the prices go. Sensibly priced for the stock in-store.

The Story Of O 5A THE CRESCENT · HYDE PARK · LEEDS · LS6 2NW
0113 275 1969

Deep in a dungeon drenched in darkness is The Story Of O. It is a far cry from the chronicles of an impoverished sex slave crippled by the shackles of love for her captor. The surroundings still hold a sensual suggestion however, as you descend into its velvety depths. An unsuspecting hair salon under the same name on Hyde Park Road acts as a smokescreen for the lascivious lair below. It's the closest you'll get to Gypsy Rose Lee's burlesque dressing room without ever visiting.

Theatrical is the incapsulating word for all that resides in this subterranea. Each flamboyant frock looks as though it has been retired to O from a life treading the boards. But these items are far from past their sell-by date. There's life in the old dears yet. High impact items find their way into the hands of David Robinson like shiny objects migrate to magpies.

Behold birdcages dripping in diamonds and pearls. Gawp at Gina couture court shoes sitting pristine in tissue cushioned boxes. Take in the turbans decorating desktops and dainty gloves displayed in every manmade shade, for The Story Of O is a wanton wardrobe that will leave you wanting more.

Look out for: The possibility of knocking something over with your bag. There is so much stuff you need to take extra care when walking around to ensure there are no breakages.

Prices: Varies from merchant, there are a [?] clothes stalls but on average i'd say £40.

Retro Boutique
**8–10 HEADINGLEY LANE · HYDE PARK CORNER · LEEDS
LS6 2AS · 0113 278 2653**

For our next excursion I need you to relax. So take a deep breath in and hold it. While gently exhaling allow the air to escape slowly, ensuring a calming sensation swooshes over you. Clear your mind and cast your thoughts to a department store dedicated solely to retro. Once the image is conjured, begin to move around the unusual and sublime that surrounds you. On your left antique furniture stripped back and given a modern makeover with bold new fabrics upholstered to the frames. To the right, a 1930s telephone sits on a dusty wooden cabinet, waiting for someone to whisper sweet nothings into it. Upstairs is a hodgepodge of hats, footwear, fabric, flags, lampshades, paintings and books. Then in a clearing there's a collection of clothing so awe-inspiring it satisfies your search-spectation and you no longer feel the need to carry on looking. Ladies and Gentlemen, welcome to Retro Boutique.

The clothes section that stole your heart in our imaginary walk through can be found on the right hand side of the store as we stroll in. Imaginative outfit choices are all down to the hard work of one young lady, Rebecca Casey. Her hand-picked clothing is colourful and flamboyant and for that reason her smallholding screams at you from the door frame amongst 19 other dealers.

This potpourri of produce has led to a plethora of adoring fans across the city swearing the boutique is the sweetest smelling shop in Leeds. So why don't you sniff it and see.

Look out for: The burlesque workshop upstairs full of vintage-style underwear, you can learn the art of the strip tease and head home with some new undies!

Prices: Jumping off point for the good quality pieces is about £45.

Upstaged 4–5 GRAND ARCADE · LEEDS · LS1 6PG · 0113 243 5855

www.upstagedleeds.co.uk

Back home in Glasgow an early Victorian arcade dubbed 'Lovers Lane' displays the largest selection of diamonds in the city. Its workmanship is elegance personified, from the tiled floors to the ornate hammer-beam roof trusses. My mall is Europe's oldest, paving the way for similar Parisian-esque arcades to pop up in our cities across the country with Grand Arcade in Leeds being one of them. Erected at the turn of the last century, it posesses the same pizzazz as my precious.

Like the largest diamond in Argyle one resident at Grand Arcade shines brightest in the bunch. Upstaged has bags of personality with gusto to boot, possessing a 'look at me' mentality without being pretentious. The clothes command a connection from the moment you make eye contact, compelling you to jump out of whatever you're wearing into what's on the hangers.

It is the 1950s that excel in here. Hand-made dresses in heavy fabrics make you truly appreciate the hours of labour that went into each piece. The art of dressing up is celebrated at Upstaged with their ethos steeped in two words: 'individual' and 'style'. The items are so authentic it can lead to heartbreak, as every true vint-a-holic

knows we're not built like those dainty dames of yesteryear. Don't worry if it's not meant to be as there's plenty more vintage left in the sea at Upstaged.

The Leeds
look book

Day

Night

BLUE RINSE

9–11 CALL LANE
LS1 7DH · 0113 245 1735
www.bluerinseleeds.co.uk

Was hard not to put this in my top three,
Blue Rinse has a subcultured coolness that
reminds me of Topshop. Mick and Jeff have
built the brand for the past 10 years, giving
it a strong identity. Best selection of men's
vintage in Leeds bar none. You'll find another
in Manchester.

RYAN'S VINTAGE

LOWER BRIGGATE
LS1 6LY · 0113 244 3090

Spit and sawdust dwelling where vintage
501s are king.

POP
12–16 CENTRAL ROAD
LS1 6DE · 0113 243 2264
www.pop-boutique.com

One of my favourite vintage chains, this little offering from the Pop family does the brand justice. Exactly what I've come to expect from Pop... perfect stock.

The Caped Crusader

WHO? Chrissie MacDougall, 33

WHAT? Nurse by day, vintage vamp by night

WHERE? Edinburgh

WHEN? Since discovering the individuality in second-hand

WHY? Because nothing compares to living like it's 1965

Chrissie MacDougall is the vintage version of Batman. Much like Bruce Wayne and his alter ego, you have no idea at first that Chrissie leads a mysterious, dual existence. Her home is the model of illusion. Tucked away in a new development christened the 'Goya Building' sits the understated dwelling of the hard-working nurse. Inside, however, it's a completely different story. Shagpile carpets, the studded leather couch, stacks of LPs and a turntable happily huddle together. You half expect Austin Powers to pop out from behind the curtains to do the Twist with Twiggy.

The *pièce de résistance* adopts the form of an Art Deco drinks cabinet, resplendent in petite, pink, mirrored tiles. The shimmering central column has a split personality, much like its sassy owner. Give it a spin and uncover another of Chrissie's secrets – the lady is a gin drinker.

Vintage is Chrissie's way of life. As a teenager she bid *bon voyage*! to the high street, opting for charity shops instead.

It was a decision her parents didn't warm to initially, insisting no daughter of theirs was going to dress like a student.

Spurred on by her growing obsession, she found a mentor in her older cousin, Elinor. More of a second mother, Elinor gifted Chrissie vintage goodies from an early age. On her last trip to Long Island, Ms MacDougall came home with more than she'd bargained for. Elinor had been upstate to nurse an elderly relative, and while sorting through Aunt Vera's belongings she came across some special pieces she knew would be perfect for Chrissie.

'I was honoured she would give me something so personal,' Chrissie says, caressing the most elegant dress I've ever clapped eyes on. 'I'm tall, so it's rare I find items that fit so well.' The Chinese-inspired gown falls dramatically to the floor, with rose gold flowers etched on its blue silk. The dress looks like it must have been made for her, even though it was bought a full 30 years before Chrissie was born.

A Girl's Guide to
Manchester

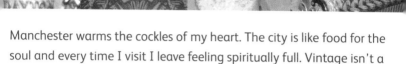

Manchester warms the cockles of my heart. The city is like food for the soul and every time I visit I leave feeling spiritually full. Vintage isn't a commodity here, it's a lifestyle, a community and most importantly, a family. You become an honorary member the moment you breach the Northern Quarter.

Meet the Parents

In every house there is a matriarch. In Manchester that icon is Afflecks. Established for over a quarter of a century, she is Queen Bee of the Northern Quarter, providing a haven for blossoming offspring. Pop, our next relative, is the cool, free-spirited cousin with a strong identity the chap you are desperate to hang out with when you're in town. This mini empire grew its roots on Oldham Street and now has boutiques across England. Then there's Rags to Bitches, the beautiful, talented little sister. She's doing things her way and rewriting the vintage bible for those seeking a different way to worship.

Look out for: The antique silver till on the third floor, still in working order.

Prices: From £5 for vintage dresses. You can't beat it!

94

Afflecks 52 CHURCH STREET · NORTHERN QUARTER · MANCHESTER · M4 1PW
www.afflecks.com · 01618 342 039

Imagine Mr Magorium's Wonder Emporium with a Tim Burton twist and you've got Afflecks. This hive of innovative activity is split over four floors with all manner of stalls and stock inside its warren-like walls. Afflecks is the Harvey Nic's of the creative world and without its presence the Northern Quarter wouldn't have thrived for the past 25 years. There's a bit of black magic at work here. I've often imagined the Victorian building and its contents caught up in a jamboree, long after they've been locked up for the night. I picture the vintage dresses swirling romantically with the antique biker jackets, the portraits of dead rock stars chatting coolly to one another, the tattoo guns trying in vain to corrupt the dainty, sewing machines, the spell only broken when the first trader opens up for a hard day's graft.

This visionary concept to create a home for fledgling entrepreneurs, artists and designers was the brainchild of James Walsh and has spawned its own fashion legacy in Elvis Jesus and Red or Dead. Here you'll uncover a barmy mix of make-up stalls, skate shops, fancy dress hirers, T-shirt vendors, tarot card readers, piercers, painters and clothes designers. Affleck purists would argue the emporium is past its heady heyday when the likes of The Stone Roses and The Happy Mondays were part of the scenery. A different breed now wafts through the double doors, keeping the place as relevant today as it was when it opened in '82.

Afflecks has a habit of nurturing future fashion superstars, so today's stallholders could be tomorrow's Wayne Hemingway. Like the finest chocolatier with a pic n mix section to salivate over there's plenty of shades and flavours to taste, from the flirty fruit and nut of the '50s to the rich dark cocoa of the 1980s. All eras are here, so suck it and see.

Prices: For £50, you'll leave with an outfit, a full belly and maybe some earrings if you are careful.

Look out for: The window display as you walk inside, it makes Barneys look amateur.

Pop

34–36 OLDHAM STREET · MANCHESTER · M1 1JN · 0161 236 5797
www.pop-boutique.com

Sunday, Monday, Happy Days is the musical memory triggered when you mosey on down to the world of Pop. It's like the 1950s on acid, vibrant hot pink and orange walls provide a canvas for religious artefacts. The Virgin Mary looms ominously over the fitting rooms beside the cash desk, crammed full of Jesus figurines. It's like stepping into a psychedelic version of *Carrie*, and much like its horror movie namesake this place has an undeniable cult status.

Pop first swung open its portals to the adoring public in 1994. Born from the Vintage Clothes Company created in 1983, Pop has since expanded from Oldham Street to stores in Liverpool, Leeds and London. The company's ethos is what makes Pop rock, as well as its fabulous vintage collection and eccentric decor. Set up by Richard Free, Pop processes over 350 tonnes of clothing annually from Europe, America and the UK. It is all about recycling and being green, long before it was deemed *de rigueur* to do so.

The vintage store, cum barbers, cum antique furniture shop, cum veggie cafe is the place to hang out for an afternoon. The staff and customers mesh together into one chilled out happy family, all conversing and having a ball in the most indulgent of surroundings. I'm always impressed by the furniture in this place and it's just as well I don't have a removal van each time I'm in Manchester or I'd be heading home with a lorry full of knick-knacks. The vintage trainer collection is really sweet as they dangle from the railing of the stairs by their laces. Also the selection of guys' vintage in here is the best I've ever come across. It's the only place I know where you can pick up some leggings courtesy of Pop's very own label, a vintage day dress, something for the other half, a hair cut and a veggie bhuna all under one roof.

Look out for: The sale rack downstairs.

Prices: Vintage starting point is between £25–30 for dresses. The bespoke dresses are considerably more, starting from £100.

Rags To Bitches
60 TIB STREET · MANCHESTER · M4 1LG · 0161 835 9265

www.rags-to-bitches.com

Old Hollywood glamour guides you around the room at Rags To Bitches. The space makes you want to call your girlfriends for an afternoon of dress up in what can only be described as an adult version of a toy box. Ornate mirrors create light and space, reflecting beautiful fabrics that have been privy to decadent decades past. A dusty pink velvet chaise longue lounges lazily in the room along with antique tables that have clusters of jewels on top of them. Vintage-inspired dresses take pride of place in the centre of the room created downstairs from re-worked fabric, others evoking the memory of yesteryear. Around the outside of the room vintage clothes are divided by colour, adding to the already luxurious shopping sensation. The fitting room is like walking into a tiny fabric-drenched boudoir, a grown-ups' den where only you and your reflection know what's going on behind the curtain.

Born of a vision via her child's Parents Night in 2003, owner Flic Everett has infused old school grace with what consumers want now. The store on Tib Street has become a trendsetter for what you can do with vintage. Flic loves nothing more than throwing parties or hosting charity balls in the shop, schoolkids can come and learn about fashion and you can even become a student yourself as Flic offers lessons on dressmaking.

Rags To Bitches is moulding itself into one of the most fashion-forward ways to shop for vintage in the UK. This place is designed to host the most spectacular pieces Flic can find, the only problem with that is it'll leave you and your girlfriends squabbling over that one-of-a-kind item you both can't live without.

Photos not from actual shop

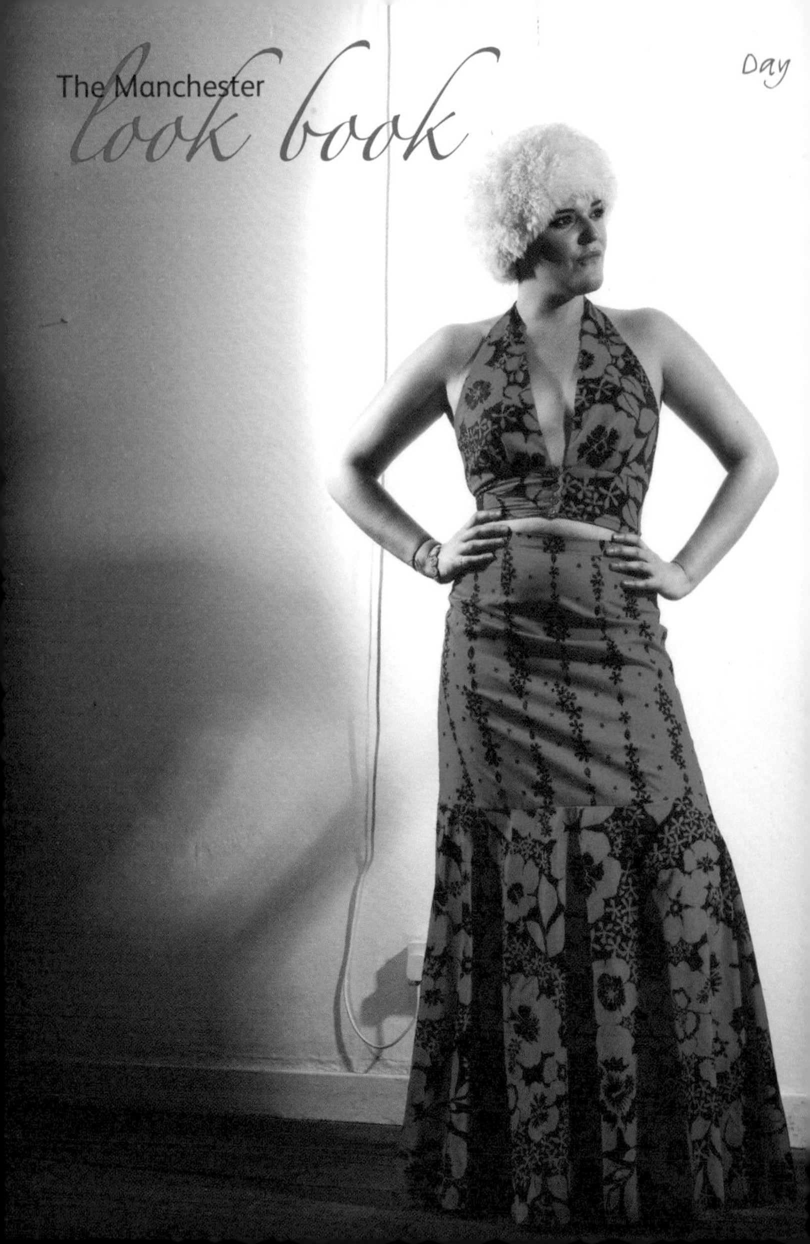

Night

BLUE RINSE MANCHESTER SHOP
31A TIB STREET · NORTHERN QUARTER
M4 1LX · 0161 832 3934
www.bluerinseleeds.co.uk

Arty arty, cool cool is what springs to mind when I hear the name Blue Rinse. They are famous for selling re-made classics. Right across from Afflecks and just before you hit Rags To Bitches you'll find flannel shirt heaven – the girls' daytime dresses are really cute in here too. There's another branch in Leeds.

RETRO REHAB
91 OLDHAM STREET
NORTHERN QUARTER · M4 1LW
0161 839 2050

Girlie chic at its prettiest, this store is sugar and spice plus all things nice. The owner gets most of her stock from the States. Displayed against flamingo wallpaper, the vintage dresses come in two flavours: original and altered. The jumpsuits are impressive here too. Everything is beautiful, which is why Retro Rehab has gathered itself a little celeb following. Shoppers include Alexa Chung and Katie from The Ting Tings.

RYAN VINTAGE
48–52 OLDHAM STREET · M4 1LW
01612 281 495

Americana vintage at its finest. This is wooden beams, spit and sawdust territory. Great selection of denim in here and I also really love the cricket jumpers, very quirky. Oodles of handbags. You have to dig in here but it is all part of the charm.

ORIGINAL OXFAM
51 OLDHAM STREET
NORTHERN QUARTER · M1 1JR
0161 839 3160
www.oxfam.org.uk

Selling the cream of the vintage crop donated to them. A top-notch effort from one of our charity institutions. Rummagers need not apply, it is precision personified. Superb selection of vintage coats. Prices slightly higher than your average Oxfam.

BEST VINTAGE
41–43 OLDHAM STREET
NORTHERN QUARTER · 0161 839 9565

For the cooler vintage cat. Retro T-shirts and shoe collection worth a look, and this store is great for the guys. Ladies, it's the rack at the back for the dresses. Staff can come across as aloof but they are just uber chilled.

AMERICAN GRAFFITTI CLOTHING CO LTD
12–14 HILTON STREET
NORTHERN QUARTER · 0161 228 3677
www.americangraffitti.co.uk

Just off Oldham Street so you don't have to trek far. Caters for fancy dress and vintage lovers alike, very colourful. They also have a concession inside Afflecks. Real mixture of stock so there is something for everyone. Check out the bargain bin.

the one that got away

The trench coat has become one of our country's biggest fashion icons. Steeped in history, it walks hand in hand with one of our oldest and most beloved fashion brands, Burberry. The creation of gabardine, the woven material trench coats are made of, by Thomas Burberry transformed the way our fashion landscape looked and over 150 years later generations still clamour for his coats. But interestingly none of this would have happened had the War Office not commissioned Thomas in 1914 to create a line of coats for their officers. It was then the trench coat was born.

I still remember the day I was introduced to my first Burberry. She was elegant in eggshell blue, with that distinct tartan emblazoned on the inside. She wasn't cut as a classic trench, which made her all the more special – it was love at first sight. The coat had been handed into the charity shop my mother works in. Mother being mother, she knew the significance of the coat and rapidly stuck five pounds into the cash register so she could bring it home to me. The tailoring on the trench was very unusual, as though it had been designed to go over the top of a '50s prom dress – plus the years had been kind to her, her fabric felt soft as butter.

Foolish spring cleaning fever swept over me one day and the love of my life went up on eBay where a bidding war commenced. Before I knew it my elegant eggshell was being parcelled up and posted to her new home in France. There isn't a day gone by when I don't think about her. Heed this warning... sleep on it before you banish your beloveds!

A Girl's Guide to
Liverpool

As part of a trio of cities that are very dear to me, Liverpool could be mistaken for a triplet – with Glasgow and Belfast completing the set. The only way of telling these three apart is from their very different accents. Their similarities boil down to this... a love of football, music, food and a very distinct passion for fashion.

Liverpool is like *A Christmas Carol*. Her streets are littered with ghosts past, present and future. Once this place touches you it will always have a prominent position in your heart.

Popular culture has carved the Liverpool we know and love today. Its mammoth musical memoir and sporting prowess floods into its sense of style and vice versa. The largest of our triplets; expect everything to be upgraded and done that little bit bigger! With a myriad of things to see, do and shop the Scousers will have you well and truly on the vintage hop.

Lurking around Liverpool's streets you'll encounter their Ghost of Christmas Past – Quiggins. Opening in the mid '80s as an antique business, it would become Liverpool's nomad, being re-homed three times. It rapidly became an epicentre for the city's alternative elite. Scousers speak so highly of Quiggins, it's like it still remains in their city centre – and I suppose it does in some guise. However the redevelopment of the area round School Lane into Liverpool ONE (their new shopping and leisure district) spelled the end of Quiggins. Forced to close their School Lane gates in 2006, many of Quiggins' former residents can be found inhabiting the Grand Central building while one of the orginal Quiggins pioneers trades under the same name on Aigburth Road.

Look out for: The bejewelled cabinet cum cash desk – I defy anyone not to leave fingerprints while looking.

Prices: Due to the nature and quality of Lessia's stock, starting prices are marginally higher – these are seriously old and outstanding pieces.

HANDLE WITH CARE

THANK YOU
THE GARMENTS
ON THIS RAIL
ARE VERY
SPECIALIZED

PLEASE ASK FOR ASSISTANCE

Somewhere In Time GRAND CENTRAL HALL · FIRST FLOOR
RENSHAW STREET · LIVERPOOL · L1 2SA

It is to Grand Central I take you next to proclaim my adoration for Somewhere In Time. The former church building has had a lot of life run through it. Originally the Liverpool Wesleyan Mission, it's also acted as a cinema and housed Liverpool's Philharmonic Orchestra as well as trying its hand as a bar and nightclub. Now the ostentatious exterior acts as a disguise for what's inside. Head into the bowels of the building to uncover a neon underworld not too dissimilar to that of the afterlife in *Beetlejuice*. Here little shops are carved out of perspex boxes as you ricochet from one plastic cube to the next. Vintage mingles with new designers, record stores and tattoo artists but the real heart-stopper is one level above the entrance.

With the basement brimming full of sinful debauchery, two flights above its head a completely celestial sanctuary awaits – Somewhere In Time is truly divine. This is where vintage vagabonds finally come to rest as Lessa Jones' place of work meshes earning a living with exhibiting. The shop has an air of the past flowing through it. Frocks from the turn of the last century have polite 'handle with care' signs attached to their fragile fabrics. Christian Dior litters the room like Eva Peron herself had just dropped off her collection.

Garments from Victoriana to the '50s are in pristine condition hanging inside plastic protectors. Mannequins go beyond the stage of showcasing clothing to having a touch of the museum on their sides. Each item that Lessa has decided to deck her store out with could be taken home as a capsule piece to have a wardrobe created solely around it, they are so eye-catching and original. Then just when you think your walk in Lessa's world has peaked the vintage wedding dresses raise your blood pressure well above the safety rate. Even if there is no significant other in your life these dresses will have you rushing down Renshaw Street, picking the first person you see and proposing, they are simply that perfect.

Look out for: The antlers, that isn't a euphemism for something — I really mean antlers.

Prices: £30-40 will see you walking away with a belter of some sort.

Raiders Vintage 38 RENSHAW STREET · LIVERPOOL · L1 4EF
01517 092 929

A hopscotch across the road from Grand Central is our Ghost of Christmas Present. Raiders Vintage is ra-ra skirts meets boho chic with a tinge of '80s edge for good measure. You will feel compelled to stay and hang out in this hot spot. Cosy leather sofas, soft silk roses and sweet little tea cups create a relaxed and funky atmosphere to mosey around in. Kelly Reid is the mademoiselle at the helm of this charming boutique. With a fine vintage pedigree behind her, this store is young and fresh with a lot of fashion-led vintage to be had hanging on the rails. Kelly's mother before her ran a vintage store across the Mersey in the Wirral and now she follows in her footsteps.

 Everything I love about city hopping for vintage is right here in this shop. Kelly's bold stock choices are very reflective of the styles you see slinking around Liverpool. The scouser look is very distinctive, sensual and loud. It is the kind of clobber to be noticed in, and if there is one thing I love about a Liverpudlian lovely, it's their vivacious fashion sense.

Shoe fiends will revel in the court displays, boots are parked under tables and dressers as if they were right at home and flamboyant frocks – to be worn without coats – can be found tarting up the surrounds. That leads me nicely to the fabosh array of funky knitwear that Kelly has picked up for all those serious vintage fashionistas out there. Mohair, cashmere, sequin-encrusted, bedazzled cable knits with geometric prints swing sumptuously together, most of them looking like they have come straight off the manufacturing line. Keeping wool brand new has always been a mystery to me as I only have to look at a washing machine while wearing one and it shrinks!

Look out for: That mural I was telling you about.

Prices: £30-40 will get you something truly scrumptious.

Little Red Vintage

74 BOLD STREET · LIVERPOOL · L1 4HR · 01517 036 872

Liverpool's Ghost of Christmas Future belongs to the bubbly owner of Little Red Vintage – Kate Harris. The girl and her store are as bright as the shop title, with Ms Harris giving Merseyside a little bit of what they've become accustomed to on the glamour front.

Bold Street couldn't be a more fitting home for Kate to have put Little Red as the store certainly lives up to the street name. This is full-on Liverpudlian glamour at its best – a look that is completely unique to the natives. Chandeliers that appear to be made out of dolly mixtures dangle from the ceiling, bringing a look I've dubbed 'girlie chic' to the property. Instead of paintings hanging from the walls it's a mural that decorates the shop – well I did tell you they liked to do things bigger round here! The mural is an ode to all things Parisienne but the clothes are an homage to the past greats of Liverpool. It would appear Cilla Black's illustrious wardrobe has been bottled – from her '60s swing dresses to '80s sequin fests – to create Little Red's stock.

Liverpool is a living, breathing oxymoron. The two best words to describe the city's look is trashy glamorous. Wag culture has nowt to do with *Wives and Girlfriends* and everything to do with stepping out the front door with your best foot forward.

Some of Kate's personal style has wangled its way onto the clothes hangers with unique party pieces having a strong presence – but it's her love for the winter wardrobe that makes things really interesting round Red. 1960s and '70s winter warmers make Kate tick so don't be surprised if you spot the odd woolly number during warmer months.

The Liverpool

look book

Day

Night

The List
Liverpool

OXFAM ORIGINALS
35–37 BOLD STREET · L1 4DN
0151 709 6739
www.oxfam.org.uk

Find genuine vintage and designer pieces in excellent condition, plus you get that feel-good factor when leaving with something since you know you've just donated to charity!

RED CROSS SHOP
36 RENSHAW STREET · L1 4EF
0151 707 1074
www.redcross.org.uk

You'll find everything from vinyl to retro bed linen – perfect for making some vintage dresses.

FLASHBACK BOUTIQUE
54 WHITECHAPEL · L1 6EG
0151 707 8231
www.flashbackboutique.co.uk

Everything is beautiful from the tiled floor to the glass dragonflies on the wall. You'll find sophisticated vintage and outrageous party pieces in here – and the staff are so lovely.

Support

WHO? Michelle Mone OBE

WHAT? Entrepreneur and creator of Ultimo

WHERE? In every town and city across the UK

WHEN? Since 1996

WHY? Because the woman is a bra tycoon

What lies beneath? We are consumed by that question. From the secrets of the Holy Grail to going behind the scenes of our favourite music videos, human nature will always want to delve that little bit deeper. When that question applies to an outfit, many images can flash before our eyes – after all no one wants to suffer the humiliation of a wardrobe malfunction. Underwear has the power to make or break an outfit! As Michelle Mone knows only too well.

The underwear mogul has revolutionised the way we think about what lies beneath – she has lifted us from the shackles of bad underwear to unveil gravity-defying cleavage even in backless frocks! Her empire was created after she was made redundant back in 1996, thanks to an uncomfortable dining experience in a not so pretty bra. The lady still holds the record for the biggest bra launch the UK has ever seen. It's easy to see why with an ethos that centres around support and comfort, her designs and aesthetics are important but really the technology has to come first. Her brand is

like a euphemism for herself; 'You can have a pretty bra with frills and lashings of lace that looks just beautiful, but if it doesn't fit well or provide you with the right support it's useless.' The woman is beautiful, but she has a brain in that gorgeous head of hers.

Ultimo is a symbol of our generation, a future vintage hall of fame-er. So when posed with the question of choosing a piece from her previous collections that will stand the test of time Michelle didn't hesitate in anointing the Miracle Plunge Bra with such an honour. 'I think vintage trends always surprise you – a few years ago we never would have predicted that conical bras would be back and considered so stylish. So I really couldn't predict, but I would definitely say that our Ultimo "Miracle Plunge Bra" will stand the test of time. It's been our best seller for over 10 years now and is hands down the best cleavage boosting bra design on the market – Julia Roberts even wore it in *Erin Brockovich*. Styles go in and out of fashion, but cleavage will always be something valued as a symbol of femininity.'

A Girl's Guide to

Sheffield

Something special is happening in the city of steel. It has broken free from its industrial shackles and morphed into a hub for hungry minds. The student population has almost doubled in the past decade, giving the place some well deserved rejuvenation. A hum of creativity coils itself around the city as new buildings spring up among old. Slick, shiny architecture slams home Sheffield's steel roots and showcases the beauty of buildings past. It is no surprise to me that Sheffield's vintage is in sync with this creative movement. The selling of secondhand is treated differently in this neck of the woods. Old rags rejected by time have been lovingly remastered in the hands of genii manipulating moth-eaten cloth into masterpieces. Much like the city itself.

Nouvelle Vintage

Sheffield is the birthplace of what I'm dubbing Nouvelle Vintage: the creative merging of old with new. Deeply embedded in Sheffield's sub-culture is a quest for individuality with a wicked artistic streak to boot. Bonding old and new isn't something that has just materialised. It has been around for decades with each generation forging a new sense of style as they go. The main difference between Sheffield and the rest of the country is how they're going about it. They are taking tired, old materials and sewing new souls into them with a cheeky nod to the past and one eye on the future that's so unashamedly now.

Prices: From £1

Look out for: The record shop in the back.

Flock Vintage and Fashion Boutique 53 HOWARD STREET

SHEFFIELD · S1 2LW · 0791 234 4001 · www.flockboutique.co.uk

Propped above a quaint Tudor-esque boozer on Howard Street adjacent to the train station, Flock is settled high up in the eaves. At the side of the building a sneaky doorway waits patiently to be entered, its content discreetly tucked up a staircase as people bevy below its floorboards. Flock is *Flowers In The Attic* meets 'Girls Just Want To Have Fun' – minus the Catholic schoolgirls and creepy mother imprisoning her children. Scaling the stairs with a touch of trepidation, doubt descends as you question your current location. After all, what are the chances of a vintage shop being on top of a pub? Thoughts of burly landlords booting you out on your backside make each step more delicate, determined not to alert anyone to your presence. Edging closer, that evocative scent so unique to vintage puts your mind at ease as you reach the summit, for right in front of you is girlie nirvana.

You'd be forgiven for thinking a teenage Sarah Jessica Parker had just pirouetted past you, spandex in tow, as she shows off her dance moves to Helen Hunt, since the place looks like a scene from their cult '80s chick flick. The bust hanging near the cash desk brings you back to the Naughties with a touch of the Gagas about it, convincing you this must be the place she got her style inspiration from. For here lies the elusive craze of Nouvelle Vintage, the merging of both worlds and the future of vintage boutiques in Sheffield.

A relatively new venture for Ms Becki Lockwood, Flock opened its side door in the summer of '08. Flock mixes some truly dainty specimens with its predominantly '80s stock. But that's not all you'll find under Ms Lockwood's roof as hand-knitted berets made by Becki's nan go with handmade embroidered T-shirts, accessories and reworked vintage clothing courtesy of Becki's mum, Christine. This family affair permeates the air, making each visit feel like you're right at home.

Look out for: The ceramic flying ducks behind the cash desk.

Prices: Starting from £15–18 for daywear.

Bang Bang Vintage
19 WESTFIELD TERRACE · SHEFFIELD · S1 4GH
0114 272 4842 · www.bangbangvintage.com

Your mission, should you wish to accept it, will only be complete once you leave Bang Bang Vintage with bags a-bulging.

If you've ever fantasised about how it would feel inside Charlie's office as his Angels take orders then I'd suggest Bang Bang to be the place to satisfy such curiosities. 1970s leather armchairs mixed with geometric wallpaper scream 'Good morning Angels... Good morning Charlie' but don't let the decor fool you, Louise Whitehead has more to offer than an Angels revival.

Smack bang by the front door is Bang Bang Recycled. '70s and '80s cocktail dresses are reshaped and styled into perfect hybrids of now and then. The vibe here is short and tight for ultimate statement dressing. Old print scarves are stitched into bandeau dresses. Reworked frocks are woven to phenomenal standards, you can even ask to have something nipped and tucked from elsewhere in store if you so desire. In the middle of the floor gold gilded frames show off the joys hanging inside. These frames aren't just any old shop fittings, these are eBay won, ex-Harrods display shop fittings bagged by Louise's own fair hand.

At the back of the store is a handbag collection that will have you quivering. Outside the fitting rooms colour-coordinated handbags in every shade a girl could wish for are crammed inside the square compartments of a white wooden cabinet. Then to the array of belts spread out on a table top, just toying with you to come for a play, after all you never know when something needs a good belting. Daytime vintage is done extremely well at Bang Bang, there is even a wide representation of guys' stock at the back of the store which is well worth a nosy.

Once read this information will self-destruct in 5...4...3...3...1.

Look out for: That impressive Levi's collection and the Mickey Mouse on the wall.

Prices: £30 or there about will get you one of their quirky tracksuit tops.

Freshmans
6–8 CARVER STREET · SHEFFIELD · S1 4FS · 0114 272 8333
www.freshmans.co.uk

Britpop is alive and well at Freshmans. It oozes cool from the moment you rock up at the front door to the minute you part with the cash at the till. This one's for the boys. The place looks like a band swap shop with jeans, lumberjack shirts, football tops, tracksuits and a fierce selection of guys' footwear all under one roof. Bucking the trend of ladies first, at Freshmans us gals have to walk through the men's gear to get to our section. Not that I'm complaining, there's a great view to behold on the way as band types trod round the aisles ploughing their way through clothes. The selection Paul has to offer is staggering and it has to be said, in all my vintage travels nowhere does men's vintage better on the UK mainland than here.

The 501s collection alone will leave you needing a tea break, it's such a mammoth task to manoeuvre. Which is no great surprise seeing as the proprietor Paul Lincoln's own personal collection exceeds the hundreds, making him somewhat of a local celebrity as it's landed him in the press several times over the last few years. Asked if he'd ever part with his beloved denims, you get the impression you have just blasphemed in front of his baby.

When you finally find your way to the ladies, you will uncover the quirkiest selection of vintage in Sheffield. The '60s and '70s are well represented in the rails designated to womankind. And so we're not left out, hangers full of cut-off jeans give the impression Mariah Carey's cast-offs have all winged their way here for our perusal. Back in the good old days when MiMi's wardrobe consisted solely of the denim shorts/strappy vest combo of course. Freshmans has a too-cool-for-school attitude, it's the kind of place you are likely to bump into the Sunny to your Cher, the Sid to your Nancy, the John to your Yoko. It doesn't get more rock'n'roll than that.

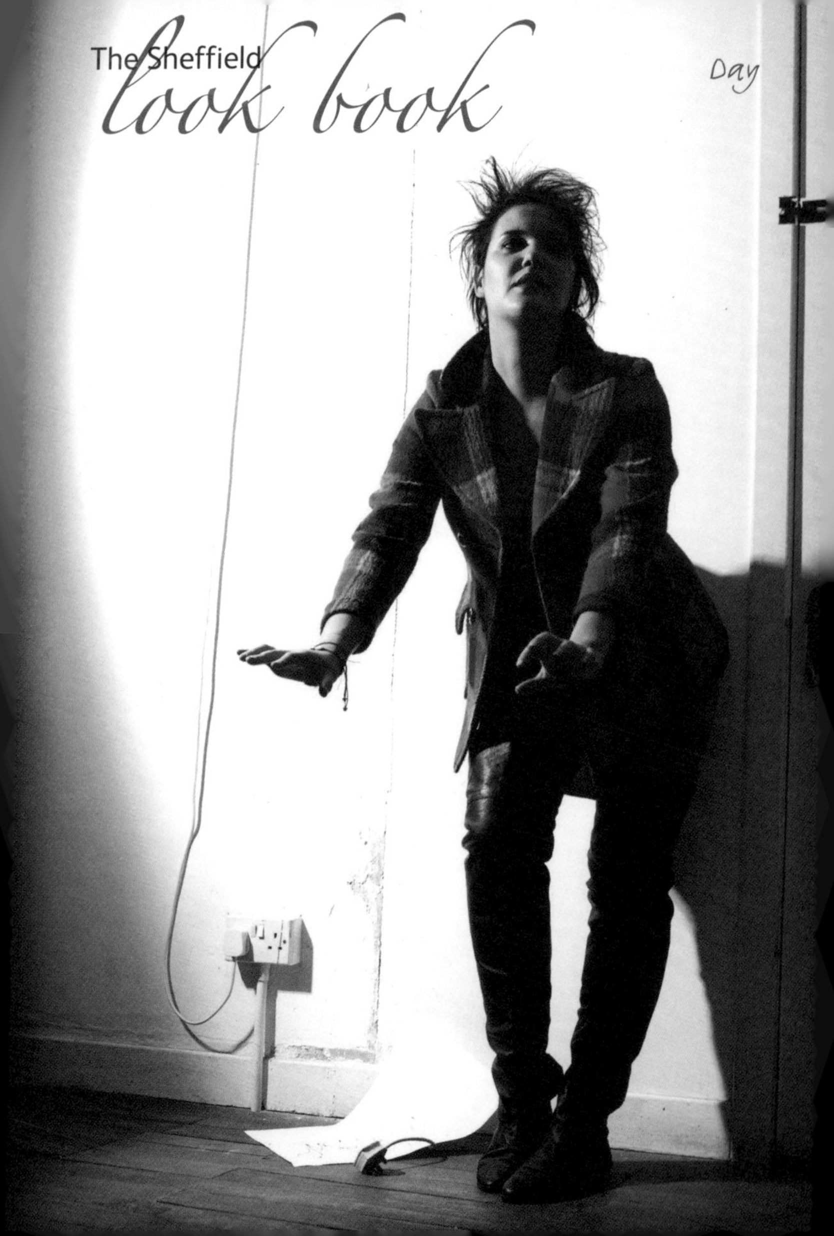
The Sheffield
look book
Day

Night

The List
Sheffield

SYD & MALLORY'S BOUTIQUE
UNIT 10 · THE FORUM
127–129 DEVONSHIRE STREET · S3 7SB
www.sydandmallory.com

This place is all about making one-off pieces without the designer price tag. They marry old fabrics with new designs in very exciting ways. The store is so quirky and a joy to be in. Plus the staff are fantastic which really sets this place head and shoulders above other independent boutiques. Definitely a spot for the individual.

A Girl's Guide to
Nottingham

The Queen of the Midlands proves there's so much more to Nottingham than men in tights. The city has been sculpted into five bite-size zones, and vintage is celebrated in each nugget; from Castle to Royal, Victoria to Broadmarsh and all the way down to Lace Market. The best of Watson Fothergill's handiwork is displayed around each district. One of my personal favourites, the Nottingham Express Offices on Upper Parliament Street, is smack bang in the middle of the vintage trail. So let it be the focal point as it guides you around. Nottingham is so aesthetically pleasing I honestly don't know what is more distracting, the clothes or the buildings.

Charlotte's Web

The lace city's vintage web is so intricate you will happily remain entrapped, spinning from one spot to the next for as long as it takes to untangle yourself. Castle Zone starts you off as Robin Hood's bow and arrow point the way to Derby Street and Celia's Vintage Clothing. Follow Derby Street downhill to the Royal Zone and standing in the shadows across from the theatre, Backlash Clothing takes centre stage. Finally Lace Market waits patiently for you to make an appearance as Upper Parliament Street turns into Lower, leading you right to the boys at The Vintage Warehouse. Zigzag from zone to zone safe in the knowledge there is no giant spider waiting to get you – however you might bump into The Sneinton Dragon if you're lucky.

Look out for: The sunglasses display at the bottom of the stair, it's where Jackie O meets Kanye.

Prices: Mostly within £20-40 average.

Celia's Vintage Clothing 66–68 DERBY ROAD · NOTTINGHAM
NG1 5FD · 0115 947 3036 · www.celias-nottm.co.uk

In an underground bunker below a fancy dress shop I can report that the 1940s are alive and well. Mannequins modelling the best in war-time allure stand frozen in time, waiting for you to leave so they can resume their post-Blitz tea party in peace. You have to catch yourself as you squeeze through narrow alleys lined either side with stock as you begin to look for the eccentric Betty Slocombe, for Celia's Vintage Clothing has more than a touch of the *Are You Being Served*s about it.

The basement has two very different identities, each bursting with personality. The first falls into the mould of the iconic British sitcom. The other is like being morphed into Hugh Hefner's wardrobe, the Barbi Benton era. Smoking jackets and dinner suits take up Hef's side, while outre outfits and cocktail dresses from the '60s, '70s and '80s display Barbi's personality in the section of the shop furthest from the stairs. Here a bunny suit would not be out of place.

To think this collection is sprung out of Celia's love for antique linen makes the journey through her downstairs parallel universe all the sweeter. Three decades on, her empire sprawls over three floors, catering for dress-up on the first, the attic for storage and the basement for vintage. Celia's store houses an enormous selection of '40s and '50s paraphernalia and it's the most impressive I have come across in the UK. If you've ever stopped and asked yourself why there is such a drouth from said period, it's probably because Celia has it all stashed away downstairs.

Look out for: The coat selection at the back of the shop goes on for decades.

Prices: Beaded and silk pieces are more expensive than daywear, on average £30.

Backlash Clothing 2 NORFOLK PLACE · NOTTINGHAM · NG1 2AA

0115 924 1455

Reincarnation perfumes the air at number 2 Norfolk Place and it's not just because you'll find vintage running through it. Prior to Eve Coup moving her robes into the room it was a dance studio and jewellers, and the presence of past proprietors can be felt as you pass by.

Near two massive windows which flood the room full of light, a bolted-down safe tells the story of its first resident as it sits peculiarly out of place in the middle of the floor, reminding everyone of the luxuries it once imprisoned. The sheer size of the space shows off how good it would have been as a dance studio. Light and airy like an expensive Manhattan loft, lazy fans spin overhead, circling at a snail's pace, trying in vain to cool the next Darcey Bussell as ghosts of dancers past twist in tutus below its weak wafts.

Hidden from view in an alley opposite the Royal Theatre, Backlash is blink-and-you'll-miss-it shopping. It's easy to walk past mid-gab with girlfriends, snubbing one of Nottingham's top spots, but once you know it's there everything else around it disappears and the joint sticks out like a vintage sore thumb calling

forth all fashionistas. Its breathe-easy browsing with friendly banter keeps you coming back. The impression that this is an extension of Eve's collection at home permeates the loft as unusual selections cross your path. This is highlighted in her assortment of Asian dresses. That delicate yet hard-wearing silk spun with vibrant colours and patterns takes you to a realm far from the gates of Nottingham.

Look out for: The massive mirror as you first step inside, it's truly beautiful.

Prices: From as as little as £5 up to £50.

The Vintage Warehouse 82–84 LOWER PARLIAMENT STREET
NOTTINGHAM · NG1 1EH

Enter the flea market of the new millennium. The place Pixar must-have taken a field trip to in preparation for making *WALL-E*. The Vintage Warehouse has all the appeal of a *marché aux puces* with a splash of futuristic flair. Found at the bottom of a long road taking you from Backlash on to Lower Parliament Street, the residents have in their midst a couple of newbies. Don't mistake their fresh-facedness for being wet behind the ears, these boys are wise beyond their years. For them, vintage is all about being green and recycling. Ben and Greg met at university, setting up their vintage venture shortly thereafter in 2007. Now no one can remember a time when the duo weren't around.

Embedded nicely into Nottingham's vintage sub culture, The Warehouse has granted itself two very large thumbs up from the city's cool elite. The hanger is a mass of activity as uber trendies bounce from one bundle of clothing to the next. Inside and out the place does exactly what it says on the tin. It's a warehouse. Exposed concrete floors, industrial lighting and bare brick sets the tone. To the untrained eye it looks like a dumping ground with piles of rubbish everywhere. In your imagination you can see wee WALL-E working relentlessly through piles of junk, whistling his show tunes as he works.

What's really refreshing about The Warehouse is how back to basics it is. This is vintage without the bells and whistles. You won't find colour-coordinated, over-priced vintage in here. It's roll your sleeves up, get on your knees, hunt for a bargain stuff. Hand-painted signs hang on wire over mountains of clothing telling you the price range for said stock. It's organised chaos at its best. Digging around you'll find yourself trying to find flaws, after all there has to be one, right? Wrong! The boys bring a no-smoke-and-mirrors attitude to the warehouse that is the cherry on top of this vintage-shaped sundae. To make things extra sugary sweet it's cheap as chips too.

Night

The List
Nottingham

Hitting Mansfield Road is a must when you are in Nottingham. It is walking distance from the city centre and well worth the detour. The street is littered with cool little eateries, independent stores, great buildings and three of Nottingham's most quirky vintage offerings. It was tough not putting these guys in my top three because quite frankly they are tremendous. So technically what I'm about to share are my top three outwith Nottingham's designated zones.

KATHLEEN & LILY'S
205 MANSFIELD ROAD · NG1 3FS
0115 941 2327
www.kathleenandlilys.co.uk

This place is like a little cupcake. Sweet, light and girlie is what to expect at Rachael and Jenna's humble abode. Named after the duo's grandmothers, the store is an homage to the women that taught them how to 'make do and mend'. The girls have a selective range of vintage, some of which has been altered and clothes that have been made by local designers. The girls are a credit to the vintage fold and their grannies.

DAPHNE'S HANDBAG
67 MANSFIELD ROAD · NG1 3FN
0115 924 0550

Eccentric only describes half of the madness
at Daphne's. Glass cabinets everywhere
ensure that you are extra careful when
looking around. You'll find furniture,
telephones, belt buckles, bags, boots, shoes,
rugs, clothes and paintings. A really fun place
to visit.

PAST AND PRESENT
7–9 FOREST ROAD EAST · NG1 4HJ

A mixture between an old army barracks
and Death's disco. Sublime to the surreal
can be had in here. Lots of military/army garb
for the boys as you walk in the front door,
head through to the women's for a mixture
of '70s to present-day second-hand. It is
Past and Present's peculiarities that makes
it pukka.

COW
2 GEORGE STREET · NG1 3BE
0115 958 3133

Part of the legendary chain. Expect
impeccable quality, really friendly staff who
know their stuff and some great shoes. I love
the quirky layout in this branch. Well worth a
walk round.

Peek-a-Boo

The moment Emily came face to face with cream moss crepe perfection she knew it was going to be a good day. She picked up her car boot sale find, only to be frozen to the spot as the Ossie Clark label presented itself. Quaking, she knew she had to pull herself together to ensure this car boot trophy was coming home. And home it came, bagging Mr Clark's masterpiece for £25! If only she'd known then the role it would play in her life, maybe she wouldn't have sold it to her best mate...

Vintage has always done it for our Emily. She turned her back on the music biz at the dawn of the '90s, packing in her record company job for life on Portobello Market. With her mum and sister in tow, the trio went from strength to strength. Before long the ladies claimed Kylie and Kate Moss as their clients as well as equipping editorial shoots with show-stealing vintage stock. From there Topshop came a-calling. Now Emily supplies their biggest store with the delightful party pieces she has become synonymous with.

Selling beautiful items had become second nature to Emily. So when her best friend Jane came knocking for the Clark car boot find she didn't think twice about selling it to her. After all, she could visit her dear Ossie and she knew it was going to a home that loved it just as much as she. Then came the proposal. Instead of thoughts of love and honeymooning all Emily could think about was getting her hands on Ossie to walk her down the isle. That was five years ago and the dress is still hanging up in Emily's wardrobe – much to Jane's disgust!

A Girl's Guide to

Birmingham

Britain's boldest building belongs to Birmingham. The Bullring typifies Birmingham's unshakable sense of style and it's the reason why navigating our nation's second largest city is such a doddle. The building encapsulates an animalistic rawness that runs deep through the heart of the city, keeping it hip but gritty. Its reconstruction has seen it become a focal point, easing all navigation around the urban jungle.

Come with me... And you'll be... In a world of pure imagination... Take a look... And you'll see... Into Birmingham's mini vintage nation.

Your golden ticket will be delivered once you've turned your back on the bull. Only then will a path appear, pointing you down Digbeth. A peek around Paul's stall at The Rag Market will sufficiently set off your vintage sweet tooth for smooth sailing on to the heart of Birmingham's vintage community – The Custard Factory.

Look out for: There's a real
mixture of sights and smells
but i'm a fabric freak so check
out the yards of clothes just
waiting to be turned into
something fabulous.

Prices: Rocky jackets range
from £25–30.

St Martins Rag Market
EDGBASTON STREET · BIRMINGHAM

B5 4RB · 0121 464 8349 · www.ragmarket.com

Like Moses parting the Red Sea, a trip straight down the middle of 'The Rag' is exactly what you want to do upon entering St Martins Market.

Sometimes the best surprises are found in the strangest of spots. From the outside The Rag looks like a community centre void of any vintage bullion – but inside there is treasure to be had. Originally named The Smithfield Market, The Rag was opened in 1817. Today it sits snugly behind the Bullring and is dwarfed by it in comparison, looking much more David next to the silver-disked Goliath. The regenerated Rag Market reopened its doors in 2000 after receiving a face lift alongside the Bullring, but its old fashioned roots are still displayed in the stalls that inhabit the grounds. A belter of a venue, the rag has bundles of character. Markets like these used to be ten a penny across the country but now they seem to be drying up. It's a crime that they are disappearing because personality like this should be preserved.

The market provides perfect pickings for people who like extremes. Fresh fruit and veg can be consumed alongside burgers and chips. Reams of fabric can be bought by the metre while newly-made dresses supply the anti DIY crowd. Dotted in between the fake hair and mountains of make-up, second-hand traders provide a haven for us vintage types. There standing amongst this mish mash is the nutty professor of vintage – Paul.

Trading for over 20 years, the collection at Paul's stall will have purists salivating. With textures and patterns a plenty, it would leave any designer desperate to clutch their pens and start drawing. Antique red military jackets gawp at you from on high. Army paraphernalia is crammed beside washed-out denim jackets. Rocky Balboa appears to have donated all his leather jackets with sheep's wool lining to Paul's cause. Tartan, furs and leopard print reign supreme, mixed with sports tops just to add a little extra eccentricity.

Look out for: The 'Oh My Love' Range.

Prices: From as cheap as £5 for daywear and starting around £10 upwards for evening. Court shoes from £4–8.

Cow

82–85 DIGBETH HIGH ST · BIRMINGHAM · B5 6DY · 0844 50 40 400
www.wearecow.com

In middle England there is a dispute over four cows. Favour one over another and you could be hurling yourself into some very hot water. Manc's will go mental in Manchester, the Steelys will come over all stern in Sheffield and everyone in Nottingham will not be impressed if you don't say their cow is the best. So I'm taking quite a big risk revealing my allegiance, not to mention the threat of being cow-patted the next time I'm in another territory! Luckily for me the cow rivalry is a friendly one so I can proclaim my heart belongs to Birmingham.

I uphold the belief that vintage is truly individual but it is facinating to see many of our vintage vendors have the same ideas on how a store should be laid out and decorated. Up and down our fair land, by the power of retro osmosis, shops appear to have commandeered the same style.

However there's a handful of folk who do things differently and the crowd at Cow are amongst them.

If I didn't know any better I'd put my mortgage on *The Crystal Maze* being conceptualised from this store. There is something industrial about the space, with exposed iron beams and shutters, rails of stock as far as the eye can see and funky robotic looking mannequins that are not quite of this world. There's always a touch of trepidation upon entering, for at any moment you half expect the legend that is Mr Richard O'Brien to slam the door shut behind you while shouting instructions to snare the dress of your dreams in under a minute. Fail this task and you'll end up entombed inside the Industrial Zone forever, letting your team mates down and forfeiting a crystal which is worth five seconds inside the dome! Then again the thought of being trapped inside Cow for all eternity isn't such a bad thought since they have stock deliveries every four to six weeks.

Custard Factory Flea Market

COME AND FLEA FOR YOURSELF

CUSTARD FACTORY

Look out for: The oldest pub in Birmingham in the grounds of the Factory, along with the massive sculptures peppering the place.

Prices: Very variable from pennies to pounds depending on attending during the market or shopping inside Urban Village.

Urban Village@The Custard Factory

GIBB STREET · BIRMINGHAM · B9 4AA · 0121 224 7777 · www.urban-village.co.uk
www.custardfactory.co.uk

The British Empire was said to be founded on its yellowy goodness and now the home of custard wraps its arms around the arts. At one time The Custard Factory held 1,000 workers with Sir Alfred Bird, its inventor, their Willy Wonka. The sprawling five acre plant was The Bullring of the 1800s. Now this British institution is fulfilling a new role within its community by serving as one of the most exciting venues in the country.

 Home to artists, designers, photographers, magazines, production companies, bars, publishing houses, crafts, restaurants and the meanest man/tree sculpture I have ever seen, The Custard Factory is the place to be and be seen.

At the weekend it bursts into life with a flea market that has such pulling power people come from all over to peruse it. During the week the atmosphere is dialed down to laid back, and even though the shopping potential isn't at its optimum the vibe is much more to my liking. Here you will find the sweetest edition to The Factory: Urban Village. Aptly titled, this little village holds several vintage concessions all individually run but equally integral to each other. Its esoteric mix has something for all but there are a couple of girls whose clothes are contagious. Cocoblack Vintage run by Angie McIntosh and Melrose Vintage by Kimberly Wincott have a real idiosyncrasy that is tapped into their own personal style and exposed in their clothes. It is always amazing to see what people pick to sell to the public and why they gravitate towards their choice and it is the girls' spirits that makes their choices special. Then there's the guy I like to dub The Candyman – Frankie Johns. Creator of all he surveys, Frankie is the man responsible for Urban Village and has been doing vintage much longer than he cares to remember. He has hooked up the likes of Supergrass and Ash with vintage threads for photoshoots – it would be fair to say he is the new Willy Wonka of The Factory.

The Birmingham
look book

Night

hat-a-tat-tat

Accessories have the ability to take an average outfit and transform it into a masterpiece. We are spoilt for choice with bags and shoes but there is one item that sits head and shoulders above all accessories – literally – and that is the humble hat.

Sally-Ann Provan is a millinery maverick who taps into vintage values to create her contemporary ranges. Her hats are like little pieces of art for your head that curve in and out of your wardrobe irrespective of time or fashion.

Concepts for a collection come initially from a colour palette. Once the colours are chosen the line falls right into place. But there was one collection that bucked that trend, when Sally-Ann came face to face with an 1970s wide-brimmed powder-blue hat in a charity shop. Instantly she was flooded with thoughts of Faye Dunaway in *The Thomas Crown Affair* and a collection was born.

But if there is one hat that sums Sally-Ann up it would be her Cameo range. Quirky yet utterly stylish – the hats give a nod to the past with their classic cameo prints etched onto wool-felt while managing to stay zeitgeist.

These hats are made with love to stick by you through thick and thin, sickness and in health, til death do you part.

www.sallyannprovan.co.uk

A Girl's Guide to

Cardiff

Misty water coloured memories – the the way we were variety of course – always come rushing back whenever I muster up thoughts of the red dragon. Precious childhood holidays now give way to vintage vacations in one of the most laid back spots in the country. Wales has spawned some of the most sensational members of our sisterhood and for that reason I love to dub Cardiff Capital of the Diva. From Charlotte Church to Catherine Zeta Jones (plus her Oscar), not forgetting Queen of all Divas Dame Shirley Bassey herself, Welsh wenches certainly have a flair for fashion that highlights the finer things in life.

Prepare to be razzle dazzled in the city of arcades and even more amazed by how vintage is delivered here – for it is a forager's dream. If you love to riffle through artefacts and antiques in old cavernous buildings while shopping for vintage then Cardiff is your spiritual home. One of our smaller cities, Cardiff rams home that famous saying 'good things come in small packages'.

Look out for: Anything that could be breakable – this place is fabulously cluttered so watch your step.

Prices: Hats go from £10 upwards.

The Pumping Station PENARTH ROAD · CARDIFF · CF11 8TT

029 2022 1085 · www.the-pumpingstation.co.uk

A feeling I belong to the wrong century frequently flits across my mind. It intensifies significantly whenever I encounter Victoriana. There is something about the craftsmanship of the period that bewitches me. Thoughts of ladies dressed to the nines simply sitting around the house all day tantalises my imagination. With Queen Victoria at the helm everything fitted this illusion of grandeur – bravado that tickles me pink. From the dizzy heights of society right down to factory workers on the shop floors, everything was geared towards aesthetics. This is why The Pumping Station is such an unique and special place to visit; it's not just about the goods that are traded under its corrugated roof. It's what the building represents, a living breathing example of how we used to live and work. It is a museum cum art gallery cum purchaser's paradise.

From Cardiff Central get yourself onto Penarth Road and turn away from the city centre. You may feel like you're being pulled out of town and off the beaten track but once The Pumping Station is in sight it will be worth it, believe me. The old water works sprawls over three floors crammed to the rafters with all sorts. Mirrors, antique doors, garden furniture, tea cups, toys and mattresses – they're all great spectacles but none as spectacular as the Dame of the water works…

Antoinette Antiques is home for ladies with serious hat fetishes, and I doff my cap to its owner Antoinette Masterson. In her possession you will find the largest vintage hat collection here in the UK, with over 800 to peruse. Sweetheart necklines and full skirted dresses Grace Kelly would have been honoured to wear add a touch of glamour to the old water works along with wedding gowns that would make you weep. The quality of the stock is so exceptional it's as if you've just hopped into Michael J Fox's DeLorean heading back to 1952 and bagged yourself a large selection of clobber fresh off the production line! If you want to get yourself 'back in time' then this is the easiest way to do it!

hobo's
60's & 70's
clothing

Look out for: The retro shop fixtures hanging on the walls.

Prices: Vary depending on night or day outfits and decade, on average £40.

Hobo's Vintage 26 HIGH STREET · ARCADE · CARDIFF · CF10 1BB

029 2034 1188 · www.hobosvintageclothing.co.uk

It's rather fitting that *Life On Mars* (the TV show, not the Bowie classic) found its way onto our screens via a Welsh intervention. After much heartache and knock-backs from every man and his dog the series was eventually commissioned by BBC Wales. No great surprise to me or anyone else who has visited Hobo's down High Street Arcade since it's like walking directly onto the programme's set. Now it may be wrong to surmise but I'm convinced the show has a lot to thank the Cardiff store for, even if there is no connection that vintage magic appears to have rubbed off.

Paint-splashed walls in orange and yellow radiate that '70s glow from corner to corner. The decade when The Clash and clashing were crowned king can be heard loud and clear as colours and clothing cry out in clamoer. Hobo's, the love child of Ben and Louise Downing, was set up in 1994 after both spent childhoods jumble sale rummaging. For pocket money Ben would get on his bike and cycle round church halls buying and selling old clothes. Now he's like Cardiff's very own version of Mohammed and the mountain – the clothes come to him. And we're not talking any old tat either. Connected better than a Mafia Don, Ben's contacts deliver him delights from Ossie Clark to Biba. The key to getting your hands on such vintage gold is simple – you need to build up good relationships with the clothes' previous owners – and build Ben has done.

Sportswear and evening-wear play the role of ebony and ivory, going together in perfect harmony. Side by side on the shop floor along with '60s purses and retro shoes, you can tell the co-owners' partnership works on and off the premises. One of Hobo's major plusses is how friendly and laid back it is, before you know it an afternoon has vanished – but you'll leave feeling like it was time well spent.

CHOICE SELECTION OF SILVER JEWELLERY

Prices: Proper antique prices for special things, but £30 can go far in here.

Look out for: The top floor — it has great views over the city. Also opening times, the market is only open Thursday to Saturday.

Jacob's Antique Market WEST CANAL WHARF · ST MARY STREET
CARDIFF · 029 2039 0939

A glimpse of old Cardiff can still be spotted amidst the shiny new buildings of Callaghan Square. The *Rocky* theme tune trumpets in your ears while heading towards the building best known as Jacob's Market. You might catch a glimpse of Joe Calzaghe sweating up a storm while running round the retro bricks, for there's fighting spirit in the old dog yet. This inveterate industrial fortress survived the bulldozing bullies of the '90s because of its usage as an antique market.

For the past 30 years and over four floors the building has seen all walks of life breeze through. It's this that makes the market so magnetic, enabling the building to act like a giant rechargeable battery that gives and takes energy. In some bizarre twist it's almost as if the bricks and mortar have fed off the energy of people passing through, stored that energy and used it as a pulse of its own. That pulse gets stronger with every visit, warning off those who threaten to tear it down. I've often wondered what walls would say if they could speak – I'm betting the market would have more than a few tales to keep you tantalised.

Due to the bohemian nature of the

building stalls are fluid and move around as people come and go. However you are always guaranteed various spreads of vintage splashed around the place like vibrant flowers.

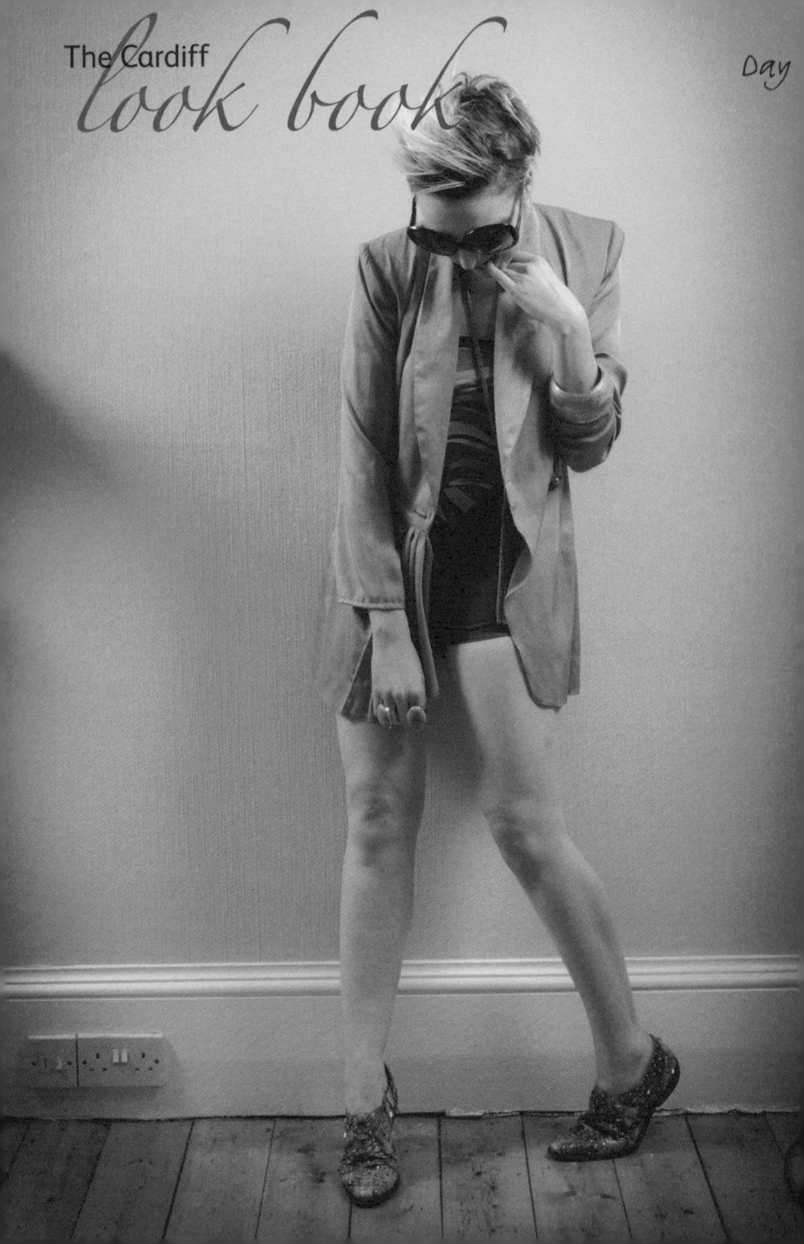
The Cardiff
look book
Day

Night

Going. Going. Gone!

WHO? Kerry Taylor

WHEN? Since 2003

WHAT? Vintage Auctioneer

WHERE? London

WHY? Because this woman's little black vintage book will have you crying with the contacts she has at hand

Every once in a while a creature so charming graces us with their presence here on Earth. Everything about them appears to be not of this world, even though they embody the human form perfectly. The culmination of their beauty, style and grace keeps us mere mortals captivated for centuries.

Audrey Hepburn was one said creature. Her effervescent beauty radiated off the silver screen, making her the bench mark for style and glamour. The legacy she left wasn't just

a back catalogue of film or her humanitarian work, she also left behind a wonderful array of clothing spanning four decades. Givenchy's muse knew what looked good on her and millions around the world wanted to emulate that... and still do. One woman knows this better than most, her name is Kerry Taylor – a lady doing the job a million vintage fiends dream of.

Joining Sotheby's in 1979 at the tender age of 20, Kerry went on to become one of the youngest auctioneers in the company's history. From there she went to work on some of the most more-ish collections to come through their doors, from celebrity outfits to royal robes. Not before long Kerry was bitten by the solo bug and set up her very own auction house, catering specifically for vintage clothing and textiles.

Outfits that have gone under her hammer have included Jerry Hall's infamous red wedding dress she married Mick Jagger in, and

Daphne Guinness's vast couture collections. Then there was the matter of Ms Hepburn's auction.

The collection of dresses came via a friendship struck up between Audrey and a lady named Tanja Star Busmann. The girls became friends when Tanja was 15, Audrey 21. Through the years a timely tradition wove its way into the women's lives – when Audrey had finished with her clothes she often passed them to Tanja, even asking

Monsieur de Givenchy to leave larger seams so they could be altered for Busmann. One dress happened to be that iconic little Chantilly lace number created by Givenchy for Hepburn in *How to Steal a Million* which went on to sell for £60,000.

There was another dress in the auction, which if it had lips, I would happily sit all day and listen to it speak. A beautiful ivory satin bridal gown created by the Fontana sisters for Audrey's planned wedding to James Hanson in 1952 that never was, a dress she was fitted for several times while filming *Roman Holiday*. It was Audrey's wish her dress should be 'worn by another girl for her wedding, perhaps someone who couldn't ever afford a dress like mine, the most beautiful poor Italian girl you can find'. That 'beautiful Italian girl' was Amabile Altobella, who went on to have an extremely happy and long marriage. Then it was Amabile's wish the dress be passed on to another bride, rather than keeping it prisoner stored in the box where it had remained for so many decades.

Kerry understands how special each individual item is that comes into her studio, she cares for them, preserves their stories and passes them on. In the case of Ms Hepburn's magnificent collection I had to ask if she felt Audrey around them while doing it. The answer was yes.

BIG GIRLS BLOUSE
UNIT 7-8 · WELLFIELD COURT
WELLFIELD ROAD · 029 2049 3800
www.biggirlsblouseuk.co.uk

Larger-than-life store, a little slice of Honolulu
in the valleys. Great for vintage replicas and
has the most adorable selection of hair clips
with flowers in every shade and style a girl
could want. Wouldn't be surprised if you end
up trying to buy Julie's (AKA Mrs Big Girls
Blouse) shoe-shaped chair.

A Girl's Guide to
London

Our country's biggest playground is connected by a Magic Roundabout. London's heartbeat loops locals around on its Underground carousel, conjoining all its glorious boroughs. The diversity of people, ethnicities, culture, fashion, food, architecture, history and nightlife is enough to keep any soul captivated for three lifetimes and I would happily devote my time here on Earth to navigating it.

Due to the sheer density of the city, London should be tackled a little differently. Instead of highlighting my top three stores I'll be divulging my favourite districts to shop for all things vintage, shouting out my hot spots as I go. This way I can maximise your shopping intake. Now who's going to argue with that?

Three is a magic number. It's why sex, drugs and rock'n'roll go so well together. It's why you wouldn't find snap without crackle or pop and it's most definitely the reason behind the success of Alvin, Simon and Theodore. A trip to London isn't complete without a peek round Portobello, Brick Lane and Camden.

Traditionally Sunday is a day of rest. Not in these parts; here it's the busiest shopping day of the week. However, if you fancy a lie in on the Sabbath don't fret about missing out on the action because this trio spring to life from around 10am. Now a word to the wise, don't let the big city fool you. London is one of the cheapest places to shop for vintage in the UK. I put this down to the wide variety of vintage to be had, so shop around. All that's left to do now is to grab a Tube map, pop this guide in your bag and plummet into the subterranean world of the Magic Roundabout.

Brick Lane EAST END

Lurking in the shadow of a chimney stack belonging to The Old Truman Brewery is Brick Lane. This melting pot of people creates one of the most diverse places on the planet to have a poke through the stalls. For centuries it's been the place where immigrants put down their roots, from the Huguenots in the 17th century fleeing France, followed by the Irish during the famine, the Jews in the mid 20th century and most recently the Bangladeshi–Sylheti community. Over the last 25 years a new breed of immigrants has settled in this colourful yet derelict part of town. A creative crowd is claiming these parts now. From artists taking advantage of the cheap studio space to new designers hiring out their first shop fronts, this clash of cultures makes for interesting cruising. Muslim men dressed in traditional garb meander alongside fashionistas frolicking in the freedom of fashion. Brilliant beigels can be had alongside the hottest vindaloo. Then there's the vintage...

Littered with the stuff, Brick Lane will leave you with frock delirium. From the market stalls at the weekend to the independent stores hawking daily, come hail, rain or shine you'll find a vintage valentine. In Hanbury Street (en route to Brick Lane), ABSOLUTE VINTAGE (15 Hanbury Street, Spitalfields, E1 6QR, 0207 247 3883, www.absolutevintage.co.uk) eagerly waits to show off its extensive shoe collection. You have never seen a selection like this in your puff. Shoes and boots from every era sit colour-coordinated in all sizes. The mini wall of fame behind the cash desk shows off the store's celeb support, displaying its vintage pedigree.

A personal favourite of mine is a tiny little store called HUNKY DORY VINTAGE (226 Brick Lane, E1 6SA, 0207 729 7387), hunkydoryvintage. com, smack bang on Brick Lane where you can bag bargains for as little as a fiver! If you're really lucky the boys will even share their Hobnobs with

Look out for: The Banksys spray-painted all round the place.

Prices: From pennies to pounds. Ranging from amazing items for under £25 to a ceiling price of around £80 in the vintage stores.

you while you try on their hand picked stock. ROKIT resides mere metres from Hunky Dory and is one of London's most beloved vintage chains, sprawling out over two stores at 101 & 107 Brick Lane (E1 6SE, 0207 375 3864, 0207 247 3777, www.rokit.co.uk).

Then there is my beloved, THE BRICK LANE THRIFT STORE (68 Sclater Street, E1 6HR, 020 7739 0242). Sandwiched between scaffolding and spectacular graffiti, this little sister to the larger store is full of eastern promise. East End Thrift Store promise that is. Down-to-earth vintage that won't leave you feeling like you've just been ripped off for someone's hand-me-downs. Believe the BEYOND RETRO BANDWAGON. It is just as good, if not better than what the locals say about it. Cheap as chips for the quality and quantity of

stock, this place would take gold, silver and bronze if it went in for the 2012 Olympics. Along the road from The Thrift Store on Cheshire Street (110–112 Cheshire Street, E2 6EJ, 020 7613 3636, www.beyondretro.com), this apogee of antique clotheries isn't the kind of place you can just 'pop in and have a look'. Going with that mentality is dangerous and will leave you carrying triple the bags on your departure plus hankering after so much more.

Portobello Road

Picture perfect in every way is Portobello Road on market day. Submerged in popular culture from cult TV classics such as *Bargain Hunt* to film royalty in *Bedknobs and Broomsticks*, this place is all you dream it will be and more. When the market is in full swing over the weekend there's really no better place to be. It is one the most aesthetically pleasing parts of London to wander through and it is most certainly the prettiest place to part with your pennies. Fashion stalls spread the length of the street, stashed in sporadic order down the strip. So if you are a devoted shopper be sure to put your walking boots on. True to its bohemian nature stalls are fluid and ever-changing but there are a couple of pitches you can count on that will always be open on market day.

My two Portobello princesses are Franny B and Emily Bothwell. They both have stalls to enthrall. You'll know when you're in front of Franny B (AKA Selina Francis-Bryden) as she is right under the West Way and her hand-painted inside-out furs will grab your attention before the bridge does. That certainly was the case when Patricia Field popped down Porty before filming season six of *Sex and the City*. Clocking the coats, she had to have one for Carrie, so the next time you are watching 'Catch 38' get acquainted with the scene where

Carrie is in a sand box eating a cookie with Charlotte while discussing children. That coat on Ms Bradshaw's back came courtesy of Ms B. Then there's the other Ms B; Emily has been down Portobello for almost two decades, but you can get to know her in a little more detail by reading her profile (page 140).

During the week the flow is less furious, giving you the full opportunity to see what's on offer elsewhere. Getting off the tube at Notting Hill Gate will lead you onto Pembridge Road, which then takes you to Portobello Road. The cluster of cool second-hand stores starts with the MUSIC AND GOODS EXCHANGE, RETRO WOMAN and RETRO MAN (all at www.mveshops.co.uk) – run by the

Look out for: The bulldog spray-painted on the side of a building above the bureau de change.

Prices: The vintage stores are obviously more expensive than what you can pick up at the market — but for designer vintage i'd go for between £40 and £150. Very special pieces will be considerably more.

same company, they are one of the oldest second-hand businesses in the country. You can get everything from music to shoes over the three stores, but it's Retro Woman that really has a go at my heart strings. Stylists and wardrobe mistresses from film sets come to swap and exchange here, so you can imagine the calibre of clobber. This is designer vintage heaven, and the prices reflect that – but don't be put off because it isn't the most expensive of stores I've ever been in. Before turning left at the end of the street onto Portobello Road, make sure you doddle into DOLLY DIAMOND (51 Pembridge Road, Notting Hill Gate, W11 3HG, 020 7792 2479, www.dollydiamond.

com), her vintage wedding dresses will have you dreaming of your own big day. When you finally find yourself halfway down Portobello, you'll come across a couple of crackers, first is ONE OF A KIND (259 Portobello Road, W11, 0207 792 5284, www.1kind. com). Don't be frightened to ring the doorbell – this store is AMAZING and not just because of its impressive A-list following, the stuff just oozes cool. Then there's MENSAH (291 Portobello Road, W10 5TD, 0208 960 8520, www. mensahvintage.co.uk), between Oxford and Cambridge Gardens on Portobello Road, this shop has something really grown up and sexy about it.

Camden

Camden is the capital of cool. It is also the spot where you'll find a little place I've dubbed the first department store of vintage. Housed inside a Victorian railway viaduct is a mini vintage village better known as The Arches at Stables Market. It's like heading into a live-in museum as history oozes out of the brickwork. The Stables no longer houses four-legged Black Beauties – in their place are cubicles crammed full of clothes, crafts and trinkets. It is such an interesting venue that once you've spent some time inside you'll be disappointed to return to pedestrian shopping.

The whole area is alive and kicking seven days a week but there's one market only open on Sundays that I'd strongly suggest you see: THE ELECTRIC BALLROOM (184 Camden High Street, NW1 8QP, 020 7485 9006, www.electricballroom. co.uk). This historic venue has held many a great gig from Oasis and The Clash to Public Enemy. It has come up against some major battles in its 70-year history and still stands to tell the tale (much to the developers' dismay!). Both the venue and market epitomise what Camden is about – the day it disappears will be the day Camden's soul is ripped out.

Making your way along the main thoroughfare of Camden High Street, feel free to snake in and out of the nooks and crannies Camden has to offer. Rokit's Camden branch, THEA (The Stables Market, Chalk Farm,

Look out for: The bronze horses at The stables, they're coming out of the walls — FABULOUS.

Prices: Can start from as little as a fiver up to hundreds of pounds. There's a budget for everyone here.

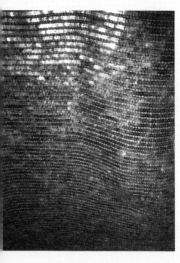

Vintage Ginas mix with Manolos, and many other shoe maestros will leave your feet feeling like they've died and gone to high heel heaven. Then head up the wrought iron stairs to the store that is all about statement dressing. It's like how George Michael felt about Club Tropicana, but instead of 'fun and sunshine' being in abundance it's 'fun and vintage'.

NW1 8AG, 020 7482 5002), a groovy vintage grotto with customised retro, new designers and impeccable vintage is back down at The Stables, along with RETRO WORLD (Arch 54, Stables Market, Chalk Farm Road, NW1 8AH, 020 7485 7656) and mini vintage emporium MODERN AGE (65 Chalk Farm Road, NW1, 020 7482 3787, www.modern-age.co.uk). Find some time to fit in my own personal favourite beside The Stables, in The West Yard where the canal takes centre stage, for there you'll encounter a double dose of BERTY AND GERTY (69 & 90 The West Yard, Camden Lock Market, NW1 8AF, www.bertyandgerty.co.uk). Shoes, boots, bags and belts can be had at ground level in their first shop.

Night

Mann

WHO? Dan Priddy

WHERE? London

WHAT? Singer/songwriter and vintage hoarder

WHEN? Since 1987

WHY? Because the man's a walking beat box whose music has featured in Nike campaigns as well as penning tracks for pop princess' The Saturdays. With a vintage collection to rival mine, Dan's the only man I ever want around on a shopping spree

The measure of creativity is originality, expressiveness and imagination. Every fibre of Dan's being possesses such qualities and it is injected into all facets of his life. From writing and producing his own music to directing and styling videos he manages to make his art look easy while other mere mortals make a mess.

Don't let Priddy fool you however, his finest talent lies in none of the above. It is the boy's ability to sniff out a bargain at 100 paces that's his real gift. This attention to detail and shrewd shopping savvy has led him to become the proud owner of a vintage selection worth salivating over. But true to Dan's form everything is given a little 'Pridding' before it's proudly shown off. Vintage buttons are sewn onto brand new jackets, jeans are altered and

everything is peppered with the right amount of accessorising.

He has a touch of the old vintage OCD. At home his wardrobe groans under the pressure of his manic hoarding; amongst his favourites you'll find his leather biker jackets and sunglasses set. He freely admits to having no idea how many of one item he has acquired. He whole-heartedly acknowledges that once he's become smitten with an item he's like a man on a mission, racking up innumerable variations of the same thing. When asked what he's going to do in the event of running out of room in his London flat (in the vain hope I'll catch some cast offs) he simply replies 'There's always space at my parents!'

A Girl's Guide to
Brighton

Brighton is so potent its seawater was prescribed to patients to cure them of all ailments. Dr Richard Russell's magic medicine soon had the masses descending on its shores as hordes of visitors flocked to sample what Brighton had to offer. I think Dr Russell was missing a trick, and though it may be true that there's something in the sea breeze here that soothes the soul and puts a spring in your step, it's the vintage that can cure anything from the common cold upwards in my eyes. The Georgians swore by Brighton and now the generation of the new millennium can't get enough of it. From the Pier to the Lanes Brighton never fails to leaves me buzzing, on each visit I'm high off its heritage and haze.

Gemini

If Brighton were a star sign that star would be Gemini. The city has two faces; romantic but sinister, youthful yet old, rough but smooth, rude while welcoming, and each side is as spectacular as the other. From its over-the-top Regency roots to its incredibly chic minimalist swagger this microcosm of differing styles couldn't represent Brighton's two façades better. The place has edge.

And it doesn't get edgier than the Lanes. Here you will come face to face with all your vintage voracity as you weave your way through one of the oldest parts of the city. It is fitting it should host such a vast vintage voice.

Our next three stops represent all facets of Brighton town: traditional, theatrical and trendy. Tuck in, it won't disappoint.

TO BE WORN AGAIN

ALL
T-shirts
£3

£10

THE SWEENEY

Look out for: Their vintage
warehouse on Providence Place.

Prices: Range from a reasonable
£20 up to £80.

To Be Worn Again   12 KENSINGTON GARDENS · BRIGHTON · BN1 4AL
01273 687811

At first glance To Be Worn Again looks like the victim of a drive-by Dayglo-ing as neon ignites the store front, spewing colour onto the cobbles. Allowing time for your eyes to adjust is necessary before entering because before you stands a sapid selection of gear that will put you in a proper partying mood. '70s maxi dresses disco with '60s sequins numbers, all of them just begging to be boogied in. The Lanes branch of TBWA was born out of the biggest vintage warehouse Brighton has to offer and the newest arrival for the clan can be found in the heart of Kensington Gardens tucked beside innumerable quirky stores, eateries and vintage bolt holes.

Opening its doors in 2009, the place has a Pat Sharp *Fun House* quality to it without a go-kart in sight. Dotted around the place are handbags, hats, court shoes, platforms and pumps. It's almost like someone has planted them there as part of the game while you wind up ping-ponging from piece to piece picking up each one up as you go.

I veered toward the store's cheery vibe because much like the two-sided city I had a sneaky suspicion all was not as it seemed on the surface. My suspicions were spot on. Many moons ago, long before vintage was king, this little place was a funeral parlour.

Bodies were wheeled in, embalmed and wheeled out. In the late '70s a new kid, who would later become a Dame, joined the street selling lovely-smelling lotions and potions. The name of her store caused quite an uproar with the undertakers the day the sign was unveiled to read 'The Body Shop'. Needless to say Dame Anita's legacy lives on while the undertakers were taken over and replaced by vintage, becoming a footnote in history.

Dirty Harry 6 SYDNEY STREET · NORTH LAINE · BRIGHTON · BN1 4EN
01273 607 527

If the sight of Clint Eastwood looming over you, Magnum in hand, slurring the line 'You've got to ask yourself one question: Do I feel lucky? Well, do ya punk?' does it for you, then vintage friends prepare to be excited. This spit and sawdust store has just the right amount of bravado to be brilliant. Americana checked shirts, cool Ts, great boots and plenty of denim on the first floor will satisfy the lads but leave the ladies thinking that Steve the owner has forgotten all about them. Don't despair over this seemingly manly approach to vintage, for one flight above your head is all you'll need to eradicate the thought you'd been forgotten.

Beside the window behind a sewing machine sits a girl threading away her blues as she remasters funky pieces of vintage. Much like in Mr Eastwood's cowboy heyday, clobber from the '60s and '70s will have you nipping out of your current clothes faster than if the movie star himself propositioned you for a nightcap. If something doesn't fit, they can make it fit down at Dirty Harry with their in-store seamstress at hand. That's not to say the alterations take away from any original beauty, all changes are done to enhance but keep the essence of the era. There's a real grit about Dirty Harry that makes it a spectacle and must-see when you're in Brighton. Plus the staff are so friendly and really get vintage. So back to the original question 'Do I feel lucky?' after a shop around Dirty Harry? It's safe to say I'd have no problem looking deep into Clint's dangerous eyes and screaming 'Yes! Yes! Yes!'

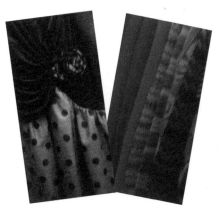

Look out for: Hidden steps and ramps, there's so much going on in this place it's easy to lose your footing.

Prices: You can pick things up for a couple of pounds. Dresses start from around £20.

Snoopers Paradise 7–8 KENSINGTON GARDENS · BRIGHTON
BN1 4AL · 01273 602 558

If Del Boy and Rodney shared a lock up at their beloved Nelson
Mandela House I'm sure that lock up would resemble Snoopers Paradise.
The sprawling indoors antiques market is as old as the Lanes themselves.
A stone's throw from To Be Worn Again this home for all things home-
less will have you tinkering around inside it for as long as you can remain
hydrated. For it is a marathon, not a sprint. Its ram-shackled quirkiness
epitomises what the Lanes are all about. Individuality. Locals would say
that it has gotten somewhat pricey over the past few years, but I think you
get what you pay for inside. The truth be told, if you don't think an item is
worth what's on the ticket then you don't have to buy it.

From the street auld Snoopers suffers from a mild case of body dysmorphia. It lures you onto the premises with a false sense that this is just another run of the mill antiques market and you'll be out in no time. As that silver spike from the turnstile grinds back into position, pushing your behind gently into the vastness, the task at hand presents itself, leaving you a little dry mouthed. So many options present themselves all at once. Go left, or turn right? Walk forward or stand still? Every item should be given the once-over since you never know what is lurking behind the Afghan rug or abandoned trumpet.

Threading through the organised chaos, rails stuffed full of clothes will appear out of nowhere, changing your direction as they show themselves. A tug of war commences between you and the crammed articles as you try in vain to peek at each outfit. Please bear in mind Snoopers Paradise is a roll your sleeves up, get your hands dirty and root around kind of place. Don't expect that '50s two-piece to be hanging immaculately waiting for you to pick it out of the pretty bunch. The best way to describe it is like mining for diamonds. You have to do a lot of work and sieve through some crap before you find your sparkler. But it makes it all the sweeter when you do.

The Brighton

look book

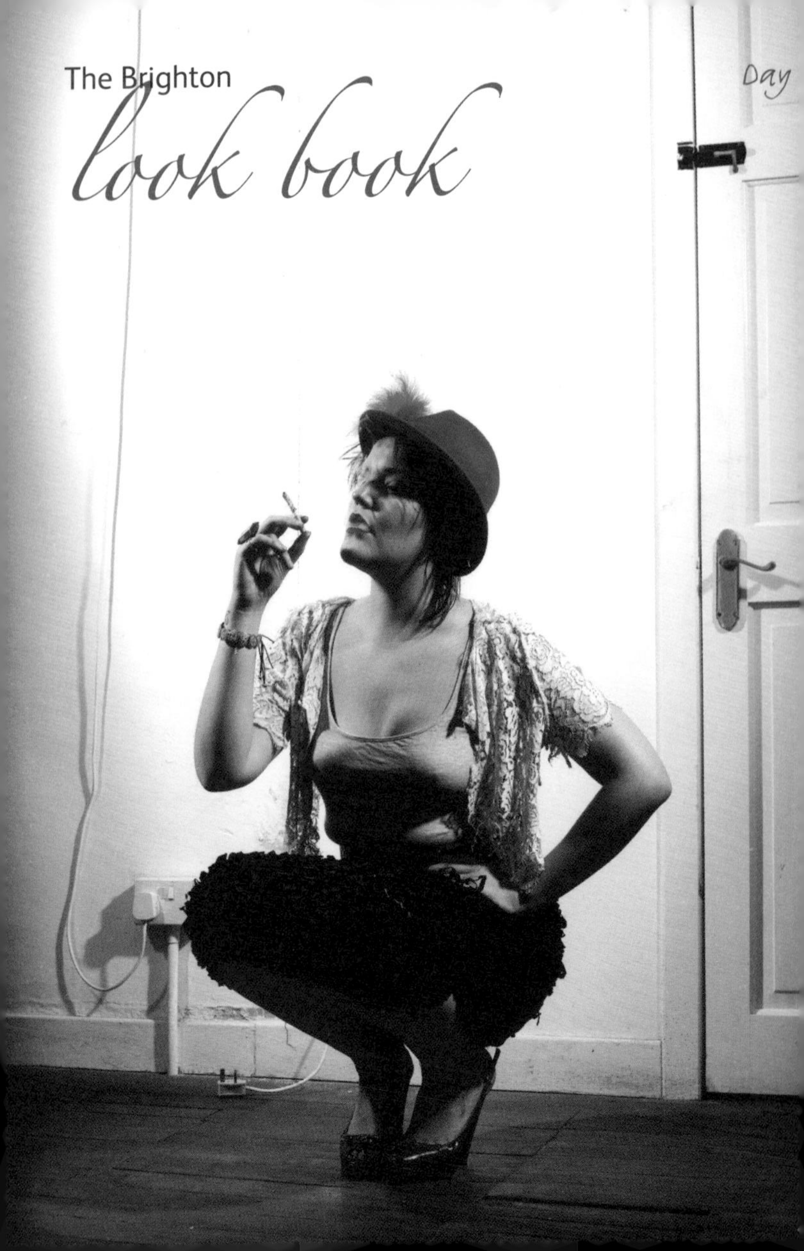

Coco De Mer

WHO? Sam Roddick

WHAT? Entrepreneur. Pioneer. Iconoclast

WHERE? International

WHEN? Since 1971

WHY? Because she does, while we wish we would...

Sometimes in life our destiny is preordained. Paths already chosen long before those first few steps are taken, it's like our genetic make-up has a master plan. It takes a little time to realise this as the stubbornness of youth blinds us into thinking otherwise – but that old saying about 'chips' and 'old blocks' wasn't coined for nothing.

Sam Roddick is said chip, convinced as a youngster a life of retail was not for her. After all, she'd grown up surrounded by the building of an empire. Her mother, Dame Anita Roddick, created The Body Shop.

Although the retailing gene didn't rub off

initially on Sam, her mother's human rights activist tendencies did. From there Coco De Mer materialised. A liberating concept that puts sexuality hand in hand with creativity. It gives sex a beauty that is rarely exposed and empowers women, exploring the concept that being visually stimulated is equally important.

With imagery influenced by Greek mythology and the Pre-Raphaelite movement, there is an Old Worldliness etched into modern photography telling stories of unleashing your inner beast.

A wise person once said that to move forward we must look to the past. Sam nods to this in all facets of her life and it is why you'll encounter vintage at Coco De Mer: "I find vintage and antiques incredibly sexy – there is a life and a mystery to the objects – the question of who made them? who owned them? what have these pieces witnessed? what love stories are sweated into their fabric? Somehow there is little to compare to the quality of the fabrics and the craftsmanship of vintage pieces – I am fascinated by ancestry and the stories of the past and how little we have evolved in terms of human nature – there is an unmatched romance to vintage pieces, that is why I believe our vintage collection has a place in my store – for the beauty, the romance and the mystery."

A small collection of her mother's '40s dresses and art deco objects and a handful of her grandmother's clothing, inspired Sam to start her own collection of '60s and '70s items. The outrageous nature of the ballgowns never fail to make her giggle – but it was a dress cast from her grandmother's hand that had most impact on Sam: "I remember putting on this dress she had made when she was in her 30s. I actually feel like I found my sexuality in that dress. It made me feel so saucy I believe that skirt taught me how to flirt – it was quite a revelation!

The List
Brighton

The Lanes are tucked away in Brighton's historic quarter and are your one-stop shop for all alternative shopping. The place is a maze of twisting alleyways offering any vintage junkie a dose of the good stuff.

Due to its bohemian nature the place is very transient and fluid with stores opening, closing and moving around its winding streets. Here's a list of some of the places I love to pop my head round when I'm in town.

HOPE & HARLEQUIN
31 SYDNEY STREET · BN1 4EP
01273 675222
www.hopeandharlequin.com

Elegance and beauty are the two words to describe Hope & Harlequin – the shop's a gem. Gorgeous vintage pieces to be had and the staff are super nice. It's impossible to walk past without going in and finding the dress of your dreams.

RED MUTHA
92 TRAFALGAR STREET · BN1 4ER
01273 603 976
www.redmutha.com

Rock and roll vintage that meets customisation with a bit of bespoke to boot. This will suit the real eclectic shoppers. This place has a really great vibe.

BRIGHTON FLEA MARKET
31A UPPER ST JAMES' STREET · BN2 1JN
01273 624 006

Classic indoor market, in the same vein as Snoopers Paradise. You can spend hours looking through tons of bric-a-brac. Good selection of vintage handbags, not so many clothes but still well worth a look.

GET CUTIE
33 KENSINGTON GARDENS · BN1 4AL
01273 693 968
www.getcutie.co.uk

This isn't vintage but it is made to measure dresses in fabulous vintage-inspired fabrics. Well worth a visit when you are in the neighbourhood.

PENELOPE'S PORTMANTEAU
42A SHIP STREET · BN1 1AF
01273 737 171
www.penelopesportmanteau.com

All about vintage accessories in here. From fur stoles to antique earrings, this place is a haven for all those whose hearts skip a beat at the mention of accessories.